THE

KETO RESET

INSTANT POT®

COOKBOOK

THE KETO RESET INSTANT POT® COOKBOOK

Reboot Your Metabolism with Simple, Delicious Ketogenic Diet Recipes for Your Electric Pressure Cooker

MARK SISSON

with Lindsay Taylor, Ph.D., and Layla McGowan

HARMONY
BOOKS · NEW YORK

The material in this book is for informational purposes only and is not intended as a substitute for the advice and care of your physician. As with all new diet and nutrition regimens, the program described in this book should be followed only after first consulting with your physician to make sure it is appropriate to your individual circumstances. The author and publisher expressly disclaim responsibility for any adverse effects that may result from the use or application of the information contained in this book.

Library of Congress Cataloging-in-Publication Data has been applied for.

ISBN 978-1-9848-2239-0
Ebook ISBN 978-1-9848-2240-6

Printed in the United States of America

Book and cover design by Jennifer K. Beal Davis
Photographs by Andrew Purcell

10 9 8 7 6 5 4 3 2 1

First Edition

This book is a magnificent team effort between the authors, their friends and families (especially the recipe testers!), and the all-star teams at Sterling Lord Literistic and Harmony Books.

CONTENTS

INTRODUCTION

BEHOLD THE CONFLUENCE OF TWO WILDLY POPULAR DIETARY CRAZES: THE KETOGENIC DIET AND THE MULTIUSE PRESSURE COOKER MACHINE! While I sincerely appreciate your interest in both, I also hope that your interest will be more than a passing fancy—that these pages will get dog-eared and sticky-noted and stained with random recipe ingredients in the years to come. I am hopeful of this possibility, or I wouldn't have tackled this ambitious project. In fact, my first instinct was to pass on the opportunity to write this follow-up book to my 2017 *New York Times* best-seller, *The Keto Reset Diet*. "Sounds interesting, but I'm too busy," was my initial reaction. Then I reflected a little more on the basic concept—keto-friendly recipes for the Instant Pot–style multiuse pressure cooker—and realized that *The Keto Reset Diet Instant Pot Cookbook* could be the perfect book for busy people who want to create healthy and delicious meals at home. It represents the height of efficiency! Not just time efficiency in the kitchen, which the Instant Pot delivers with one of the greatest modern breakthroughs in cooking technology, but I'm also talking about *metabolic efficiency*, which keto affords as one of the greatest ancient breakthroughs in dietary technology.

When the paleo/primal movement was in its infancy a decade ago, my driving ambition was to challenge flawed conventional wisdom and dispense new dietary strategies based on evolutionary health principles—eating from a list of foods that promote optimal gene expression: meat, fish, fowl, eggs, vegetables, fruits, nuts and seeds, and certain healthy modern foods such as high-fat dairy products and dark chocolate with a high percentage of cacao. This simple premise—that we evolved to thrive on these foods, and that many processed modern foods are extremely destructive to human health (especially sugars, grains, and refined vegetable oils)—has formed the foundation of the paleo/primal/ancestral health philosophy.

Thanks to the digital age, dated conventional wisdom has been shattered, and evolutionary health principles have been widely accepted and validated by respected science, as well as by millions of positive user experiences. Health-conscious folks across the globe are now highly informed about the dangers of excess carb intake and insulin production, and the benefits of ditching carbohydrate dependency and becoming fat- and keto-adapted. While we still have significant differences of opinion and debate about the nuances of healthy eating, there seems to be near-universal agreement on many important big-picture elements, for example:

- Colorful, nutrient-dense whole foods like vegetables, fruits, nuts, and seeds form an excellent foundation of healthy eating.
- Nutrient-deficient foods such as refined grains, sugars and sweetened beverages, and refined high polyunsaturated vegetable oils are extremely destructive to human health, and they are primary driving factors of today's epidemic diet-related disease conditions of type-2 diabetes, heart disease, and cancer.
- If you choose to consume animal products, choose grass-fed/pasture-raised or USDA-certified organic.
- Nourishing a healthy gut microbiome is a recently discovered and essential element of healthy eating. This is achieved by consuming ample amounts of food rich in prebiotic fiber (aka resistant starch) and/or probiotics.

Consequently, this book offers something for everyone: vegetarian selections; varied and delicious meat, fish, poultry, and egg selections; and plenty of gut-nourishing meals. All the recipes are deemed to be "keto-friendly" as they are all low in carbohydrates, with carbs coming from vegetables, dairy, and coconut products, and minimally from eggs, nuts and nut butter, and some fruits: lemons, dark berries, and avocado. (Yes, avocado is a fruit!) Or course, not every single dish by itself conforms to the generally accepted macronutrient ratios for a ketogenic diet (65 to 75 percent of calories obtained from natural, nutritious fats; 15 to 25 percent of calories from protein; and 5 to 10 percent of calories from carbs), but each of these recipes could easily be included in a well-formulated ketogenic diet. While a breakdown of carbohydrates, protein, and fat grams and calories is provided for each recipe, I caution you against taking an overly regimented approach to your keto goals. If you were to apply the keto macronutrient litmus test to every snack or meal you contemplated, you'd quickly become frustrated and eventually burned out on the whole keto deal. Believe me, I've seen it happen too many times.

Instead, I encourage you to think in terms of living a keto-friendly lifestyle (including exercise, sleep, and stress management behaviors that promote fat burning instead of sugar burning) and eating in what I call the "keto zone." This entails focusing on a general pattern of eating nutrient-dense meals, eliminating processed carbs, getting comfortable with intermittent fasting, and not obsessing about blood ketone values or tracking every gram of nutritious carbohydrates you consume.

You will occasionally see an ingredient in this book such as a beet or sweet potato that a rigidly adherent keto eater might be inclined to shun. However, these foods offer tremendous nutritional value and, in moderation, can certainly be included in a ketogenic diet. If recipes in this book do not conform perfectly to keto guidelines you've seen on the Internet, or you eat some treats that are not found in any keto or low-carb book, please embrace the idea that it's okay, that you are getting a nutrient-dense meal, and that if you have strayed from a keto path you can easily calibrate back in the direction of keto at future meals. For example, if you enjoy some delicious sweet potato fries and a fruity cocktail (or two . . .) while out with your friends one night, you can have a zero-carb breakfast the next morning, or engage in intermittent fasting (an important under-pinning of a keto dietary strategy), and you'll be back on track.

When you operate in the keto zone, your daily carbohydrate intake might range from under 50 grams per day when you are fasting or making a focused effort to sustain nutritional ketosis, to up near 150 grams when you are not in a distinct keto phase and are more liberal with your carbohydrate consumption. As I discuss in detail in my *Primal Blueprint* books and online educational courses, if you ditch grains and sugars, it's pretty difficult to exceed the primal-approved upper limit of 150 grams of carbs in a day. Even when you are hard-core keto and staying under 50 grams per day, you can still consume abundant servings of assorted above-ground vegetables (such as leafy greens and those in the cruciferous family) and land safely under 50 grams. If you are eating in a primal-aligned pattern and going up to 150 grams per day, you can also consume plenty of seasonal fruit; other nutrient-dense carbs like sweet potatoes, wild rice, and quinoa; and more liberal quantities of the incidental carbs found in nuts, seeds and their derivative butters, high-cacao-percentage dark chocolate, coconut milk, and other nutritious foods.

Living in the keto zone is about metabolic flexibility—the ability to gracefully burn a variety of fuel sources based on what your body needs at any particular time. In contrast, a high-carbohydrate, high-insulin-producing eating pattern is the essence of metabolic *inflexibility*—being inefficient at burning stored body fat, never making any ketones, and having your energy level, mood, appetite, and cognition being highly reliant upon regular doses of dietary carbohydrates. If you can't skip a meal without feeling tired, cranky, and hungry, this is an indication that you will benefit greatly from improving your metabolic flexibility by following the methodical process outlined in *The Keto Reset Diet*. Briefly, you start with a 21-Day Metabolism Reset to ditch grains, sugars, and refined vegetable oils and replace them with the foods you enjoy from the aforementioned list of ancestral foods. Next comes a fine-tuning period with fasted mornings that upregulate your ability to burn stored body fat. Finally, a focused, six-week period of nutritional ketosis follows, where you obtain the maximum body composition and the anti-inflammatory, immune, and cognitive benefits of deep keto.

Even when you choose to disengage from the strict keto parameters at some point after your six-week commitment, you will maintain a heightened level of metabolic flexibility moving forward. If you ever fall off the wagon and need to recalibrate, you will be able to turbocharge your metabolic flexibility by stringing together keto-aligned meals and intermittent fasting. The key takeaway here is that you have to progress carefully through the entire Keto Reset journey, completely disengage from the disastrous state of carbohydrate dependency, and teach your body to prefer fat for fuel around the clock. Becoming fat- and keto-adapted is believed by many medical and longevity experts to be the best way to promote longevity, minimize the risk of the epidemic diet-related diseases in modern society, and also to achieve authentic and lasting weight loss.

WHAT IS KETO, ANYWAY?

"Keto" is a catchall term for anything pertaining to the metabolic state of *ketosis*, the burning of *ketones*, or the dietary macronutrient composition (very low carb, moderate protein, high fat) that promotes the attainment of this delicate metabolic state. Ketones are an internally manufactured energy source that are used by the brain, heart, and muscles in the same manner as is glucose (sugar). They are produced in the liver as a by-product of fat metabolism when—owing to prolonged fasting or extreme restriction of calories and/or dietary carbohydrates—insulin, blood sugar, and liver glycogen levels are very low. Many people go through life never getting anywhere near this state, and never experiencing the almost magical effects of burning this natural superfuel. Ketones and fat (since the burning of these two caloric energy sources always go hand in hand) help minimize the inflammation and oxidative damage that come from eating the modern grain-based, high-carbohydrate diet. Keto awareness arises from the paleo/primal/low-carb dietary movement that has become wildly popular over the past decade, but compared with these strategies, keto is more specific with respect to required dietary macronutrient ratios—and it can be even more effective for weight loss, disease protection, and peak cognitive and athletic performance than a standard low-carb diet.

HOW TO USE THE INSTANT POT (AND OTHER PROGRAMMABLE, MULTIUSE PRESSURE COOKERS)

The recipe instructions are presented with the assumption that you are using one of the popular Instant Pot® brand machines. While "Instant Pot" has become the ubiquitous moniker for any programmable pressure cooker, there are many similar, quality products from brands like Bella, Bestek, Black+Decker, Cosori, Crenova, Crock Pot, and more. The button presentations seem to be quite consistent among the machines, so it's highly likely that you will be able to discern which button or function to use if your machine uses terms that are similar to the terms used in these recipes or descriptions. The specifics in this section relate to my unit, which is the Instant Pot Duo Plus, released in early 2017.

Multiuse pressure cookers (also called multicookers) have achieved great popularity by virtue of their versatility and ability to speed cooking time by a factor of two to six times while using 70 percent less energy. Throw some meat, veggies, seasonings, and a liquid base into your unit, and you will have a delicious stew ready in half an hour, instead of having to strategize an all-day slow cooker operation. Yes, even with a couple of pounds of tough stew meat or a whole raw chicken, your meal will be ready by the time you change out of your work clothes and take a quick shower. The pressure cooker works by locking to form a sealed air space that traps the water vapor and triples the amount of heat transferred to your meat, vegetables, eggs, or whatever other ingredients you are cooking.

Pressure cooking is especially effective for bone broth, as it coaxes the joint-boosting collagen and glycosaminoglycans, minerals, prebiotic fiber, and other lauded nutrients out of bones in record time. To make a nutritious bone broth, just save your chicken carcass or purchase some bones from a butcher—especially joints, which make the best bone broth and are also inexpensive. Throw in some spices and a few cups of chopped veggies such as carrots, celery, and onions, and cook at high pressure for 30 minutes or up to 2 hours. Yes, as little as a half hour yields fabulous, gelatinous bone broth, something that can take up to two days in an ordinary slow cooker. Bone broth aficionados must try it to believe it! With the logistics streamlined, you will hopefully make bone broth a dietary staple. A book called *The Ultimate Guide to Bone Broth* has over one hundred extremely creative and colorful recipes.

While the recipes in this book emphasize the time-saving pressure cooker method, there are also numerous recipes that utilize the slow cooker and other functions on these versatile multiuse units. The Instant Pot and other brands of multicookers are touted as being able to replace numerous other kitchen appliances, such as a stand-alone pressure cooker, slow cooker, rice cooker, egg cooker, yogurt maker, food warmer, steamer, and sterilizer, not to mention your stovetop and oven. Check out the "Fats and Fermentations" section of the book to discover some exciting ways to use your Instant Pot to make your own homemade ghee, yogurt, crème fraîche, and more. These recipes are specially designed to show you how you can use your Instant Pot to add to your diet more of the healthy fats and fermented foods that are critical to the success of your keto efforts.

BASIC UNDERSTANDING OF FUNCTIONS AND SETTINGS

The first objective is to not be intimidated by all the buttons! There is a lot happening on the control panel with the LCD screen readouts and the numerous preset buttons. Since I'm a little technophobic myself, I've prepared this section to help you conceptualize the big-picture operating principles of the Instant Pot and gain some familiarity with the buttons. I suggest that you read this section carefully with the unit right in front of you and plugged in. This way you can engage in some hands-on playing around to help strengthen your comprehension of the written material. Again, if you have a different brand of pressure cooker, or a different model of Instant Pot, you'll have to intuitively adapt the following information to align with your machine's buttons and functions, knowing that the same basic principles apply.

First, let's discuss the control panel, which comprises many buttons surrounding a large LCD screen. The buttons can be categorized as either *preset meal functions* (e.g., Soup/Broth, Cake, Egg, Porridge), *cooking functions* (e.g., Slow Cook, Sauté, Pressure Cook, Sterilize), or *settings* (e.g., Pressure Level, Delay

Start, Keep Warm, Cancel, and the plus and minus buttons). There is substantial variation in specific button placements and names among different models, but learning some general distinctions like the aforementioned can be helpful—especially when the cooking function buttons are intermingled with the preset meal buttons on many units. Frustrating, I know.

Fear not, you'll get accustomed to everything with regular use—including the fact that on several models there is no Start button! On my Duo Plus, I just program my cooking or hit a preset meal button and the machine commences cooking in about five seconds. Generally, your LCD display does a great job indicating what is going on with your machine.

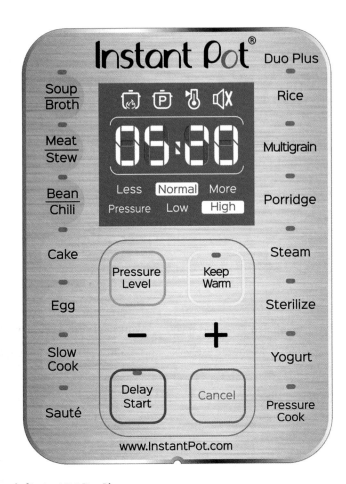

Control panel of Instant Pot Duo Plus

Before you get started, it's essential to understand the difference between Pressure Cook and Slow Cook. In Pressure Cook mode, the steam release valve on the lid is turned to the "Sealing" position. This enables the formation of the aforementioned sealed air space that speeds cooking time. The steam release valve is a small, teardrop-shaped valve in the middle of the back of the lid. It swivels back and forth between directions labeled "Sealing" or "Venting." On the Duo Plus and other units, the labels appear in raised black lettering on the black lid. What's more, the valve does not lock into place, so even when you put the valve in "Sealing" position prior to cooking, it is (counterintuitively) loose and floppy.

When a pressure cooking session is complete, you can allow the pressure to release naturally or quickly, based on your recipe guidelines or urgency to get to your food! With natural pressure release (sometimes abbreviated NPR in recipes), you allow the cooker to cool down gradually until the float valve (a tiny, round, unlabeled, recessed silver button located next to the steam release valve on the lid) drops down into its hole. In contrast, when the cooker is under high pressure, the float valve is flush with the casing around it. The gradual cooling down and pressure release in the pot may take 10 to 40 minutes depending on what you cooked. Wrapping a damp towel around the lid will speed the cooling process, but make sure that the steam release valve is not covered. When the float valve drops, you can easily open the lid and remove your meal.

You can also choose to quick-release the pressure by turning the steam release valve to the "Venting" position. You may have heard scary stories from pressure cooker users who, upon fiddling with the steam release valve, have been startled and jumped up in alarm at the sound and heat of the escaping vapor. Indeed, you'll want to avoid putting your face near the valve, and take care to keep your fingers away from the vapor trail when opening the valve. Stand back from the Instant Pot and place your fingers only on the sides of the valve, never on the top. The lid will not open until the pressure has released sufficiently.

In Slow Cook mode, the steam release valve on the lid is left open, allowing vapor to continually escape for a longer and gentler cooking time. The Slow Cook function works just like a regular slow cooker. The default setting is 4 hours, and you can adjust cooking time and temperature up or down.

Here's an overview of the other cooking function buttons:

- "Sauté" for tasks you might do in a pan on your stovetop, such as simmering vegetables and other sensitive foods, or browning meats with an open lid

- "Steam" for traditional steaming of vegetables, eggs, or pot-in-pot cooking with the food elevated above water on a rack; done under high pressure
- "Sterilize" to clean utensils, baby bottles, jars, in boiling water
- "Keep Warm," with a timer, for after cooking has completed

If you have an older model and you are feeling jealous and left out that you don't have some of the aforementioned bells and whistles, understand that your unit has almost all the same functionalities, which you can program manually. For example, you can sterilize using the Steam function on older models.

The Instant Pot touts its 9-in-1 versatility, but I believe its greatest value is as a pressure cooker. I have found better success using a traditional slow cooker when slow cooking is called for, and I often use a frying pan for sautéing; but the pressure cooker seems like one of the greatest innovations in kitchen appliances in many years. I still remember the excitement of the first Cuisinarts back in the early 1970s!

MANUAL PROGRAMMING BUTTONS

In complement to the preset meal buttons (see below), you can use buttons to manually program your cooker to the specifications of your recipe. First, choose the cooking function (Slow Cook, Pressure Cook, Sauté, Steam, Sterilize, or Keep Warm), adjust the cooking duration with the plus or minus buttons, and navigate between High or Low pressure with the Pressure Level button if you are using a pressure-cooking function. If you are using Slow Cook or Sauté, the Pressure Level button is irrelevant and thus deactivated.

Older Instant Pot models have buttons that actually say "Manual" and "Adjust," while newer models have eliminated those buttons. Hence, on the newer models, you can simply choose your cooking function (e.g., Pressure Cook, Slow Cook, Sauté), choose a Pressure Level (if applicable) of Low or High, and then adjust the cooking time with the plus or minus buttons. Most of the recipes in this book use the Manual/Pressure Cook function because it is the simplest, no-fuss setting that works for almost everything. I also like the Cancel button (displayed as Keep Warm/Cancel on other models) when you mess up and want to start over, any time, anywhere! The Cancel button is also used to switch functions in the middle of a recipe, for example going from Sauté into Pressure Cook after browning meat for a stew. The Delay Start button (aka timer) allows you to load ingredients into the cooker and initiate a future start time, so you can have a delicious meal ready when you walk in the door. (This is only available on newer models—sorry, early adopters!)

USING THE PRESET MEAL BUTTONS

These buttons are typically named after specific preparations such as soup, meat, chili, rice, porridge, and more. The preset meal buttons initiate cooking at specific recommended times and temperatures aligning with the type of food. This gives you one-touch convenience that can be touted in a product promo, but I don't use these buttons much. Keep in mind that the machine is just guessing that an average-size roast will be done after 35 minutes of high pressure-cooking for example, or trying to cook an egg at that "just right" status between hard-boiled and soft-boiled. I prefer to follow recipes with tested and proven precise cooking times, as is detailed in this book. That said, if you find the Meat/Stew button or the Egg button works perfectly for your associated recipes, great!

Note that if you hit a preset meal button repeatedly, it will cycle from the default "Normal" cooking time and temperature, to a "More" presetting, then to a "Less" presetting, and then back to the "Normal" default. For example, on the Instant Pot Duo Plus, if you push the Egg button, the LCD screen will say "Normal," with a cooking time of 5 minutes and the pressure on "High." If you push Egg again, the "Normal" LCD light will switch to "More," and the cooking time will move to 6 minutes with the pressure on "High." If you push Egg again, the "Less" light will illuminate, with a cooking time of 4 minutes with the pressure on "High." You can also hit one of the preset meal buttons and then make manual alterations to the time or temperature presets, according to your preferences (e.g., for softer eggs or rarer meat).

On many pressure cookers, the Rice function is fully automated. Cooking 2 cups of rice takes about 12 minutes at high pressure. On the units with this rice automation feature, you will not be able to adjust the time.

DEFAULT SETTINGS AND ADJUSTMENTS FOR PRESET MEALS AND COOKING FUNCTIONS

MEAL SETTING	PRESSURE SETTING	DEFAULT TIME	"MORE" TIME	"LESS" TIME
Soup/Broth	High	30 min	40 min	20 min
Meat/Stew	High	35 min	45 min	20 min
Bean/Chili	High	30 min	40 min	25 min
Cake	High	30 min	40 min	25 min
Egg	High	5 min	6 min	4 min
Rice	Low	(Automated)		
Multigrains	High	40 min	45 min soaking+ 60 min cooking	20 min
Porridge	High	20 min	30 min	15 min

Above is a quick look at the default and adjustment settings for the cooking functions and preset meals on the Instant Pot Duo Plus.

Cooking Functions

Slow Cook: Preset to 4 hours in "Normal," and also 4 hours in "More" and "Less" modes. Temperature on "Normal" equates to medium setting on a slow cooker (190° to 200°F). "More" raises temperature similar to a high setting on a slow cooker (200° to 210°F). "Less" lowers temperature similar to a low setting on a slow cooker (180° to 190°F). Plus or minus buttons change time in 30-minute increments. You must set the steam release valve to "Venting" when slow cooking, or use a slow-cooking lid that can be purchased separately.

Sauté: The default setting ("Normal") is a medium heat suitable for routine sautéing of vegetables or fish. For a higher heat, adjust to "More," which is suitable for stir-frying or browning meat. For a lower heat, adjust to "Less," which is suitable for simmering or thickening sauce. All heat levels are preset to 30 minutes and cannot be changed; this is an important safety feature! Of course you can always stop the sauté function at any time by hitting Cancel. The lid remains open during this function.

Steam: Preset ("Normal") is 10 minutes at High pressure. "More" adjusts to 15 minutes at Low pressure. "Less" adjusts to 3 minutes at High pressure. Use the metal steam rack/trivet or basket that came with your unit to raise food above the water you add to the pot insert. The lid is closed and the steam release vent is set to "Sealing."

Sterilize: Preset ("Normal") is 30 minutes at Low pressure. "More" adjusts to 30 minutes at High pressure. "Less" adjusts to 30 minutes with no pressure—a hot water bath at below boiling temperature. The lid is closed and the steam release vent is set to "Sealing."

Pressure Cook: Enables manual programming of pressure level and cooking time per recipe guidelines. Choose Low or High pressure with the Pressure Level button and the plus or minus buttons to adjust cooking time. Lid is secured and the steam release valve is set to "Sealing." This is the function that you will see called for most often in the recipes.

Yogurt: Preset ("Normal") is 8 hours to ferment milk—the first step to making yogurt. "More" adjusts to pasteurize the milk, as the next step to making yogurt. The LCD readout says "Boil" for this function. You can also use the Yogurt preset on the "Less" setting to ferment sweet rice for 24 hours to make a popular Chinese dessert called *jiu niang*.

Programming Buttons

Delay Start: Preset to 6 hours, adjustable with the plus or minus buttons. Hit this button after you have loaded ingredients and programmed your recipe.

Keep Warm: Press button to activate Keep Warm, preset to 10 minutes. The small light at the top of the button will illuminate, and the Keep Warm function will initiate after the meal program is completed, keeping the contents between 145° and 172°F.

Pressure Level: Press to alternate between High and Low pressure when using applicable pressure-cooking functions (e.g., Pressure Cook but not Slow Cook).

Cancel: Cancels any programming, illuminates "Off" on LCD screen, and turns machine off after 10 seconds.

HIGH-TECH CONNECTIONS

The Instant Pot Smart Bluetooth models have Wi-Fi capability. You simply download the Instant Pot Smartcooker App for your platform and pair your device with the Instant Pot, then operate the Instant Pot from your mobile device. You can choose one of the recipes featured in the App and start the recipe, manually program a cooking operation remotely, or program a delayed start time.

ACCESSORIZE YOUR INSTANT POT

If you use your Instant Pot a lot—and trust me, you will—you might find that the addition of a couple inexpensive accessories really enhances your ability to get the most out it. Here are the top three accessories I use most often, as well as a few honorable mentions that I think are quite handy.

1. Steamer Basket

From under $10 on Amazon

This is by far the accessory I use most frequently, whenever I am cooking something like small florets of broccoli or cauliflower that will fall through the standard trivet. There are many different options for steamers. Mine is a collapsible basket that has a hook in the middle for lifting it out when hot, but any similar model will do.

2. Silicone Cupcake Cups or Egg Bites Molds

From under $10 on Amazon

Again, there are many different sizes and styles to choose from, from individual mini muffin cups to round silicone trays that look like cupcake pans. They are inexpensive and handy, so I suggest getting a few different options. If I had to pick one, I'd get the egg bite molds with the silicone lids.

3. Stackable Stainless Steel Steamer Insert Pans

From under $30 on Amazon

This two-tier, stackable system fits neatly into your Instant Pot, so you can do pot-in-pot cooking or reheat multiple items at once. Use just one of the pans for steaming or for holding smaller vessels. This isn't really a must-have so much as a super-convenient-

and-versatile accessory. I use mine for reheating meat and steaming veggies at the same time, and for "baking," as in the Layered Lemon Cheesecake on page 172.

Honorable Mentions

Inner Cooking Pot

From under $30 on Amazon

This is simply a second inner pot identical to the one that came with your Instant Pot. If you ever make more than one Instant Pot dish in a single meal, this allows you to lift out the first cooking pot and immediately start making the second dish in a clean pot.

Springform Cake Pan

From under $15 on Amazon

Truth be told, I use this mostly for cheesecakes, but isn't that a good enough reason?

Egg Steamer Rack

From under $10 on Amazon

This one is nice if you like to make soft-cooked eggs like for the Eggs and Prosciutto-Wrapped Asparagus Soldiers on page 000, but you can also use it for hard-cooked eggs or simply as a second trivet. It will hold up to 7 eggs upright.

Gripper Clippers

From under $10 on Amazon

These clippers grip your inner pots to allow you to safely lift them out after cooking. They will also lift steamer baskets and other hot stands out of your Instant Pot, as well as hot items (up to 5 pounds) from your oven and microwave.

Extra Sealing Ring

Less than $8 on Amazon for the 6-quart ring

It is a good idea to have an extra sealing ring on hand as they can crack or develop unpleasant odors over time.

Silicone Lid

From around $10 on Amazon

Cover your inner cooking pot for transporting food to a potluck or storing leftovers in the fridge.

Glass Lid

From under $20 on Amazon

This allows you to see your food during slow cooking and other non-pressurized functions.

BEFORE YOU START

Before you get started cooking the fabulous (if I do say so myself!) recipes that follow, here are a few notes. First, all of the recipes were written for a 6-quart Instant Pot and were tested in the Instant Pot Lux, Duo, and Ultra models. Many users find that their preferred cooking times vary a bit from even the best recipes. This also happened to us, when our friends at Andrew Purcell Photography in New York City prepared the recipes for photographing. There are assorted possible reasons for this, ranging from personal preference to altitude to the ingredients you purchased. I recommend that you take notes in these pages to perfect your cooking times. By the way, if you have a unit with low-pressure and high-pressure options, assume that each recipe is meant to be cooked at high pressure unless specified otherwise.

Several of these recipes call for sautéing some of the ingredients in the Instant Pot before transferring them to a container and doing pot-in-pot pressure cooking (cooking in another container such as a baking dish or a ramekin in your Instant Pot). I wrote these recipes to be truly one-tool meals, giving you the option for using your Instant Pot from start to finish. However, you can always opt to sauté on the stovetop if you prefer.

Join the Instant Pot Facebook community of over a million members for ongoing support and creative ideas. There is even a Keto Instant Pot Facebook community with tens of thousands of members. The Keto Reset Facebook community that I formed with my teammates offers personalized support from expert moderators, lively engagement with keto enthusiasts, and comprehensive online educational courses to ensure your keto efforts are successful. Good luck with your immersion into the world of pressure cooking! Don't be afraid to experiment and even mess up now and then! Soon you will gain more confidence with the unit and get into a groove of easy go-to meals that you can enjoy even on the busiest of days.

INSTANT POT COOKING TIMES

For your convenience, here are recommended cooking times for common foods, adapted from the information provided on the official Instant Pot website. These are meant to be used as guidelines, but whenever possible follow the cooking times provided in a tried-and-true recipe. All cooking times below are in minutes.

For meats and poultry, I generally allow the pressure to release naturally for 5 to 15 minutes, with poultry on the shorter end and stews, pot roasts, and other dishes where the meat is meant to be fall-apart tender on the longer end.

Seafood and fish can easily become overcooked, so opt for an immediate quick-release of the pressure when the cooking time is up.

I generally quick-release the pressure when cooking vegetables, especially ones like squash or carrots that will become mushy if overcooked.

INGREDIENTS	COOKING TIME (IN MINUTES)
MEATS	
Beef, stew meat	20 per pound
Beef, roasts and brisket	15 per pound for small chunks 20 per pound for large chunks
Beef, ribs	20 to 25 total
Ham, slices	9 to 12 total
Ham, picnic shoulder	8 per pound
Lamb, stew meat	12 to 15 total
Pork, loin roast	20 per pound
Pork, butt roast	15 per pound
Pork, ribs	15 to 20 total

INGREDIENTS	COOKING TIME (IN MINUTES)
POULTRY	
Chicken, breast (boneless)	6 to 8 total
Chicken, whole (4 to 5 lbs.)	8 per pound
Chicken, cut with bones	10 to 15 total
Chicken, bones for stock	12 to 15 total
Turkey, breast (boneless)	7 to 9 total
Turkey, breast (whole)	20 to 25 total

INGREDIENTS	COOKING TIME (IN MINUTES)	
SEAFOOD AND FISH	**FRESH**	**FROZEN**
Crab, whole	2 to 3	4 to 5
Fish, whole	4 to 5	5 to 7
Fish, fillet	2 to 3	3 to 4
Mussels	2 to 3	n/a
Shrimp or Prawns	1 to 3	2 to 4

INGREDIENTS	COOKING TIME (IN MINUTES)	
VEGETABLES	FRESH	FROZEN
Asparagus	1 to 2	2 to 3
Beets, small	11 to 13	13 to 15
Beets, large	20 to 25	25 to 30
Broccoli florets	0 to 2	2 to 3
Brussels sprouts, whole	2 to 3	3 to 4
Cabbage, shredded	2 to 3	3 to 4
Cabbage, wedges	3 to 4	4 to 5
Carrots, sliced or shredded	2 to 3	3 to 4
Carrots, whole or chunked	6 to 8	7 to 9
Cauliflower florets	2 to 3	4 to 5
Collard greens	4 to 5	5 to 6
Greens, chopped	2 to 3	4 to 5
Leeks	2 to 3	3 to 4
Mixed vegetables	3 to 4	4 to 6
Onions, sliced	2 to 3	4 to 5
Parsnips, chunked	3 to 4	4 to 6
Potatoes, cubed	2 to 3	3 to 4
Potatoes, large (whole)	2 to 3	3 to 4
Rutabaga, chunked	2 to 3	4 to 5
Spinach	2 to 3	3 to 4
Acorn squash, sliced	3 to 4	4 to 6
Butternut squash, sliced	2 to 3	3 to 4
Sweet potato, large (whole)	3 to 4	4 to 6
Sweet potato, small (whole)	2 to 3	4 to 5
Sweet pepper, sliced or chunked	2 to 3	4 to 5

INSTANT POT BASICS

EGGS

Keto is often tongue-in-cheek called the bacon and butter diet, but it would probably be more appropriate to call it the egg diet. We keto and primal folks love our eggs! They didn't earn the nickname "nature's perfect food" for nothing. A perfectly packaged bundle of protein and healthy fats, B vitamins, choline, selenium, and other vitamins and healthy compounds that also happens to go perfectly with bacon and butter? I'll take a dozen.

EGGS COOKED IN THE SHELL	LOW PRESSURE	HIGH PRESSURE
Soft cooked (just-firm white, runny yolk)	5 min + 1 min NPR	3 min + 1 min NPR
Medium cooked (firm white, creamy yolk)	8 min + QR	4 min + QR
Hard cooked (firm white, fully cooked yolk)	12 min + QR	5 min + 5 min NPR

QR = Quick release; as soon as the Instant Pot beeps, carefully turn the steam release valve to Venting to release the pressure manually.

NPR = Natural pressure release; allow the pressure to come down on its own for the specified time before carefully switching the steam release valve to Venting.

EGGS COOKED IN THE SHELL

MACRONUTRIENTS PER 1 LARGE EGG

CALORIES: 78

FAT: 5 G/48 CALORIES

CARBOHYDRATE: <1 G/
2 CALORIES

PROTEIN: 6 G/25 CALORIES

The Instant Pot has become my go-to method of cooking foolproof, easy-to-peel eggs. Simply pour 1 cup of water into the bottom of your Instant Pot, then place a metal steam rack/trivet or a specialized egg steamer rack inside and place 1 or more eggs on the trivet. Secure the lid and turn the steam release valve to Sealing. Select the Manual or the Steam function and adjust the cooking time (see the table opposite). While the eggs cook, prepare a bowl with ice water so you can immediately transfer the eggs to an ice bath after cooking. This is especially important if you want soft- or medium-cooked yolks. When the Instant Pot beeps, release the pressure according to the specified method and move the eggs to the ice bath.

The table opposite includes the times that I have found work best for me after a lot of playing around with various cooking and steam release times. Use these as a starting guide, but understand that you might need to adjust them based on your personal preferences. I recommend that the first time you attempt soft-, medium-, or hard-cooked eggs in your Instant Pot, you start with just one as a test run.

BONE BROTH

If you have an Instant Pot and aren't using it to make your own bone broth, you are missing out on a nutritional gold mine. Bone broth is absolutely packed with vitamins, minerals, prebiotic fiber, and special compounds like collagen and glycosaminoglycans for healthy skin, joints, and connective tissue. I always have a freezer full of bone broth for making healthy soups like the ones in this book, and for drinking hot out of my favorite mug. Making it in the Instant Pot is a game changer! Instant Pot bone broth is thick and rich and done in 2 hours, compared to ten times that long in a slow cooker.

The easiest way to get started on bone broth is to keep a large zippered plastic bag in your freezer. When you are cooking and have leftover vegetable scraps such as the leaves and root ends of celery, carrot fronds, broccoli or kale stems, and so on, add them to the bag. Then the next time you roast a whole chicken, or you get some nice, big knuckle bones from your local rancher, you can have a batch going in no time.

BONE BROTH (CHICKEN OR BEEF)

MAKES 8 TO 12 CUPS (DEPENDING ON
THE SIZE OF YOUR INSTANT POT)

12 to 16 ounces beef soup bones, chicken feet, chicken carcass, etc.

2 to 4 tablespoons tomato paste (only if making beef broth)

2 to 3 cups (5 to 10 ounces) vegetable scraps or roughly chopped vegetables (see Note)

2 cloves garlic, smashed

10 black peppercorns

2 bay leaves

Fresh herbs such as thyme or rosemary sprigs (optional)

Filtered water

MACRONUTRIENTS PER 1 CUP

CHICKEN BONE BROTH

CALORIES: 52

FAT: 3 G/26 CALORIES

CARBOHYDRATE: 1 G/4 CALORIES

PROTEIN: 5 G/21 CALORIES

BEEF BONE BROTH

CALORIES: 21

FAT: 0 G/0 CALORIES

CARBOHYDRATE: <1 G/2 CALORIES

PROTEIN: 5 G/19 CALORIES

1. If making beef broth: Preheat the oven to 400°F. Place the beef bones on a heavy rimmed baking sheet. Brush them with the tomato paste. Roast for about 30 minutes until they are well browned.

2. For either broth: Add the roasted beef bones or chicken parts, vegetables and/or scraps, garlic, peppercorns, bay leaves, and herbs (if using) to your Instant Pot. Cover completely with filtered water, but do not exceed the Max line on the pot insert.

3. Secure the lid and set the steam release valve to Sealing. Press the Pressure Cook or Manual button and set the cook time to 120 minutes.

4. When the Instant Pot beeps, allow the pressure to release naturally, 15 to 25 minutes.

5. To rapidly cool the broth, plug your kitchen sink and fill it with ice water. Place a metal bowl in the ice water, and place a metal sieve or colander over the bowl. Very carefully strain the hot broth into the bowl. Allow it to chill for about 15 minutes, stirring it occasionally.

6. If desired, strain the broth again through a fine-mesh sieve into a Pyrex measuring pitcher. Pour the broth into mason jars, leaving about 1 inch of headspace. Secure the lids and place the jars in the refrigerator or freezer. Alternatively, pour the broth into ice cube trays or silicone molds and freeze; then pop out of the molds and store in a zippered bag in the freezer. Use refrigerated broth within a few days.

NOTE: If you haven't accumulated vegetable scraps, use 1 large onion, 2 celery stalks with leaves, and 2 carrots with leaves.

For paleo/primal and keto folks, spaghetti squash is one of the best options for adapting any traditional pasta dish to fit a low-carb lifestyle. Cooking spaghetti squash in minutes is one of my favorite uses for my Instant Pot. You can have perfect "noodles" in a quarter of the time it takes to roast spaghetti squash in the oven and without heating up your whole kitchen. Simply top with butter and Parmesan cheese, or with the delicious Red Sauce (page 93). Just add shredded chicken or sautéed shrimp for a complete meal.

SPAGHETTI SQUASH

MAKES 3 TO 4 CUPS

1   medium spaghetti squash

1   cup water

MACRONUTRIENTS PER 1 CUP

CALORIES: 42

FAT: <1 G/4 CALORIES

CARBOHYDRATE: 10 G/40 CALORIES

PROTEIN: 1 G/4 CALORIES

1. Carefully halve the spaghetti squash crosswise, through the equator (this is easier and safer than cutting lengthwise through the stem). Place each half cut side down and cut straight down through each half so the squash is now quartered. Scoop out and discard the seeds.

2. Pour the water into the Instant Pot. Place a metal steaming basket (preferred) or the metal steam rack/trivet inside. Place the spaghetti squash flesh side down in the basket or on the rack; it is okay if the pieces overlap.

3. Secure the lid and set the steam release valve to Sealing. Press the Pressure Cook or Manual button and set the cook time to 7 minutes.

4. When the Instant Pot beeps, carefully switch the steam release valve to Venting to quick-release the pressure. When fully released, open the lid.

5. Remove the spaghetti squash and allow it to cool for a few minutes. Use a fork to scrape the flesh of the squash into "noodles" into a bowl. It can be helpful to use a clean kitchen towel to hold the squash if it is still hot. The noodles are now ready to eat or use in a recipe.

Pumpkin might not be a usual staple of keto cuisine since it's a starchy carbohydrate, but I like to use it in moderation in soups, stews, or smoothies, or to make the occasional homemade pumpkin spice latte (not the sugar bomb you'll get at your local coffee shop). It has an excellent nutritional profile and a little goes a long way for flavoring. If you have an Instant Pot, it is incredibly easy to make your own pumpkin puree, which you can then freeze in small portions to use later.

PUMPKIN PUREE

1   small pie pumpkin

1   cup water

MACRONUTRIENTS PER ¼ CUP

CALORIES: 40

FAT: 0 G/0 CALORIES

CARBOHYDRATE: 10 G/40 CALORIES

PROTEIN: 1 G /4 CALORIES

1. Use a sharp knife to carefully cut the pumpkin into 3 or 4 large pieces. Cut off and discard the stem. Scoop out the seeds and strings. (Save the seeds to roast later!)

2. Pour the water into the Instant Pot. Place a metal steaming basket (preferred) or the metal steam rack/trivet inside. Arrange the pieces of pumpkin flesh side down in the basket or on the rack, overlapping them to fit. Secure the lid and set the steam release valve to Sealing. Press the Pressure Cook or Manual button and set the cook time to 20 minutes.

3. When the Instant Pot beeps, allow the pressure to release naturally for 10 minutes, then carefully switch the steam release valve to Venting. When fully released, open the lid. Carefully remove the pumpkin. It might fall apart a bit, which is not a problem.

4. Use a spoon to scoop the flesh away from the skin. Discard the skin and use a potato masher or blender to puree the flesh. Store the puree in an airtight container in the refrigerator. Freeze any puree you do not intend to use within a few days. You can portion the puree into small mason jars for freezing, or you can freeze it in silicone molds or ice cube trays. If you do the latter, once frozen, pop the puree out of the molds or trays and store in a zippered bag in the freezer.

Perhaps one of the most visible signs that the low-carb movement has officially gone mainstream is that you can find riced cauliflower in the produce and freezer sections of most grocery stores now. The convenience can't be beat, but it's obviously not as fresh as making it yourself. The Instant Pot offers the best of both worlds—fast *and* fresh! Once it is cooked, you can add fats like butter or extra-virgin olive oil, and any herbs or spices you want; or you can use the rice in another recipe.

CAULIFLOWER RICE

MAKES FOUR TO SIX 1-CUP SERVINGS, DEPENDING ON THE SIZE OF THE CAULIFLOWER

1   cup water

1   medium head cauliflower

MACRONUTRIENTS PER 1 CUP

CALORIES: 20

FAT: 0 G/0 CALORIES

CARBOHYDRATE: 4 G/16 CALORIES

PROTEIN: 2 G/8 CALORIES

1. Pour the water into the Instant Pot. Place the metal steam rack/trivet inside. Place the whole cauliflower on the rack.

2. Secure the lid and turn the steam release valve to Sealing. Press the Pressure Cook or Manual button and set the cook time to 2 minutes.

3. When the Instant Pot beeps, allow the pressure to release naturally for 5 minutes, then carefully switch the steam release valve to Venting. When fully released, open the lid and transfer the cauliflower to a cutting board. Allow it to cool for a few minutes.

4. When it is cool enough to handle, cut it into florets. Working in small batches, place the florets in a food processor and pulse until it reaches the desired consistency. Transfer it to a bowl.

BONUS RECIPE:
GOLDEN CAULIFLOWER RICE

2 tablespoons coconut oil or ghee

¾ teaspoon ground turmeric

¼ teaspoon curry powder

¼ teaspoon ground black pepper

¼ teaspoon sea salt

1 batch Cauliflower Rice (opposite)

¼ cup slivered almonds (optional)

1. In a large skillet, heat the coconut oil over medium heat. Add the turmeric, curry powder, pepper, and salt and cook, stirring constantly, until fragrant, 1 to 2 minutes. Do not allow the spices to burn.

2. Add the cauliflower rice and stir very well to completely coat it with the oil and spices. Cook, stirring, for about 1 minute. Taste-test the rice. Adjust the salt if needed and cook longer if you want softer rice.

3. Just before serving, stir in the slivered almonds, if desired. Serve warm.

MACRONUTRIENTS PER SERVING

NO ALMONDS

CALORIES: 96

FAT: 7 G/61 CALORIES

CARBOHYDRATE: 8 G/32 CALORIES

PROTEIN: 3 G/12 CALORIES

WITH ALMONDS

CALORIES: 141

FAT: 11 G/95 CALORIES

CARBOHYDRATE: 9 G/38 CALORIES

PROTEIN: 5 G/19 CALORIES

BREAKFASTS

40

45

48

50

54

58

60

These are great for busy families and busy mornings. Make a triple batch on Sunday and store them in the fridge or freezer to quickly reheat during the week.

SAUSAGE AND KALE EGG MUFFINS

MAKES 2 SERVINGS

1   teaspoon avocado oil

2   teaspoons bacon fat (or more avocado oil)

4   ounces fully cooked chicken sausage, diced (see Note)

4   small kale leaves, any variety, finely chopped

½   teaspoon kosher salt

½   teaspoon ground black pepper

4   large eggs

¼   cup heavy whipping cream or full-fat coconut milk

MACRONUTRIENTS PER SERVING

NO CHEESE
CALORIES: 333
FAT: 31 G/279 CALORIES
CARBOHYDRATE: 3 G/12 CALORIES
PROTEIN: 11 G/44 CALORIES

WITH CHEESE
CALORIES: 390
FAT: 36 G/324 CALORIES
CARBOHYDRATE: 6 G/24 CALORIES
PROTEIN: 15 G/60 CALORIES

1. Use the 1 teaspoon avocado oil to grease the bottom and insides of four silicone muffin cups (preferred), ceramic ramekins, or half-pint mason jars. If you have a silicone egg bites mold, you can also use that for this recipe.

2. Set the Instant Pot to Sauté and melt the bacon fat. Add the sausage and sauté for 2 minutes. Add the chopped kale and ¼ teaspoon each of the salt and pepper. Sauté until the kale is wilted, 2 to 3 minutes longer.

3. Meanwhile, in a medium bowl, lightly beat together the eggs, cream, and remaining ¼ teaspoon each salt and pepper.

4. Press Cancel. Divide the kale-sausage mixture among the four muffin cups. Pour the egg mixture evenly over the kale and sausage and stir lightly with a fork. If desired, top each with 1 tablespoon shredded cheese. Loosely cover the cups with foil or silicone lids.

5. Pour the water into the Instant Pot. Place the metal steam rack/trivet inside. Place the four muffin cups on top.

6. Secure the lid and set the steam release valve to Sealing. Press the Pressure Cook or Manual button and set the cook time to 5 minutes.

7. When the Instant Pot beeps, allow the pressure to release naturally for 10 minutes, then carefully switch the steam release valve to Venting.

4   tablespoons shredded white cheddar or Swiss cheese (optional)

1   cup water

8. Carefully remove the muffins from the Instant Pot. Serve hot or warm.

NOTE: You can use any variety of sausage you want for this recipe. Low-sugar breakfast sausage (4 small links) or mild or spicy Italian (1 large link) work well. If using pork sausage, cook it according to the package directions before starting this recipe.

Frittatas are fantastic, but they can be tricky to prepare on the stovetop. Using the Instant Pot removes some of the logistical challenges, so you can rotate this into your breakfast game more often. Serve this frittata with a dollop of guacamole or sour cream for added healthy fats.

HAM AND PEPPER FRITTATA

MAKES 2 SERVINGS

2 tablespoons avocado oil

¼ cup chopped onion

¼ cup finely chopped green bell pepper

¼ cup finely chopped red bell pepper

½ pound cooked ham, cubed

6 large eggs

½ cup heavy whipping cream or full-fat coconut milk

½ teaspoon sea salt

¼ teaspoon ground black pepper

¼ teaspoon dried basil

¼ teaspoon dried parsley

¼ teaspoon red pepper flakes (optional)

½ cup shredded cheddar cheese (optional)

1 cup water

MACRONUTRIENTS PER SERVING

CALORIES: 708

FAT: 50 G/450 CALORIES

CARBOHYDRATE: 11 G/44 CALORIES

PROTEIN: 51 G/204 CALORIES

1. Use about 2 teaspoons of the avocado oil to grease a stainless steel, Pyrex, or silicone baking dish that fits inside your Instant Pot. If your metal steam rack/trivet does not have handles, make a sling (see Note).

2. Set the Instant Pot to Sauté and heat the remaining oil. Add the onion and bell peppers and sauté for 3 minutes. Stir in the ham and sauté for 2 minutes to heat through. Press Cancel.

3. In a medium bowl, whisk together the eggs, cream, salt, black pepper, basil, parsley, and pepper flakes (if using). Pour this mixture into the prepared baking dish. Quickly stir in the ham, onion, and peppers. If desired, sprinkle the cheddar over the top. Cover the dish with a metal or silicone lid, or use foil.

4. Pour in the water. Place the steam rack/trivet inside and arrange the sling over it so the two ends stick up like handles, then lower the baking dish onto the sling and rack.

5. Secure the lid and set the steam release valve to Sealing. Press the Pressure Cook or Manual button and set the cook time to 35 minutes.

6. When the Instant Pot beeps, allow the pressure to release naturally for 10 minutes, then carefully switch the steam release valve to Venting. When fully released, open the lid. Use the sling to carefully remove the baking dish. Serve hot.

NOTE: To make a sling, pull off a piece of foil about 18 inches long. Fold it in half lengthwise and then in half again lengthwise.

Don't recoil at the title! This manly man–style preparation is my Instant Pot take on an incredibly unique and tasty dish invented by my old friends, the notorious primal-living Curley brothers. Because it is so filling, it's great after a long hike or strenuous session in the gym.

ALMOND BUTTER GROUND BEEF BOWL

MAKES 4 SERVINGS

1 tablespoon avocado oil or coconut oil

1 pound grass-fed ground beef

1 clove garlic, minced

½ teaspoon sea salt

½ teaspoon ground black pepper

½ teaspoon ground turmeric

¼ teaspoon ground cinnamon

¼ teaspoon ground coriander

¼ teaspoon red pepper flakes, or more to taste (optional but recommended)

¼ cup almond butter

½ cup full-fat coconut milk

1 small head green cabbage, shredded (or a 12-ounce bag shredded cabbage or slaw mix)

MACRONUTRIENTS PER SERVING

CALORIES: 574

FAT: 42 G/380 CALORIES

CARBOHYDRATE: 15 G/59 CALORIES

PROTEIN: 35 G/140 CALORIES

1. Set the Instant Pot to Sauté and heat the oil, swirling the pot to coat the bottom. Crumble in the ground beef and cook for 3 minutes, breaking up the meat with a wooden spoon or meat chopper.

2. Stir in the garlic, salt, black pepper, turmeric, cinnamon, coriander, and pepper flakes (if using).

3. Add the almond butter and coconut milk. Stir constantly until the almond butter melts and mixes with the coconut milk. Layer the cabbage on top of the meat mixture but do not stir.

4. Press Cancel. Secure the lid and set the steam release valve to Sealing. Press the Pressure Cook or Manual button and set the cook time to 4 minutes.

5. When the Instant Pot beeps, carefully switch the steam release valve to Venting to quick-release the pressure. When fully released, open the lid and stir the meat mixture. It might be a little stuck to the bottom because of the almond butter. If so, give it a good scrape with a wooden spoon.

6. Taste and adjust the salt and black pepper, and add more red pepper flakes if desired. Use a slotted spoon to transfer the mixture to a serving bowl. Serve hot.

I don't know about you, but I'd rather do something else with my Sunday morning than wait 45 minutes at a trendy breakfast spot, especially when I could have this preparation done in less time than it would take me to get a table!

CHORIZO BREAKFAST TACOS

MAKES 6 SERVINGS

2	tablespoons avocado oil
1½	pounds fresh chorizo or links with casings removed
¾	cup sour cream
½	cup chicken broth
6	large eggs, washed
	Large lettuce or cabbage leaves to use as taco shells

TOPPINGS (OPTIONAL)

½	cup shredded cheddar cheese
¾	cup mashed avocado
2	tablespoons finely chopped fresh cilantro
	Chile-lime salt (like Tajín)

MACRONUTRIENTS PER SERVING

NO TOPPINGS
CALORIES: 695
FAT: 59 G/531 CALORIES
CARBOHYDRATE: 4 G/16 CALORIES
PROTEIN: 35 G/140 CALORIES

WITH ALL OPTIONAL TOPPINGS
CALORIES: 793
FAT: 67 G/599 CALORIES
CARBOHYDRATE: 10 G/41 CALORIES
PROTEIN: 38 G/153 CALORIES

1. Set the Instant Pot to Sauté and heat the oil. Crumble in the chorizo. Sauté for 2 minutes, breaking up the meat with a wooden spoon or meat chopper.

2. Stir in the sour cream and broth.

3. Place a long-legged metal trivet directly on top of the sausage mixture. Place the eggs on the trivet.

4. Press Cancel. Secure the lid and set the steam release valve to Sealing. Press the Pressure Cook or Manual button and set the cook time to 10 minutes. Meanwhile, fill a medium bowl with ice water for the eggs.

5. When the Instant Pot beeps, carefully switch the steam release valve to Venting to quick-release the pressure. When fully released, open the lid. Use tongs or a large spoon to transfer the eggs immediately to the ice bath. Stir the chorizo mixture and allow it to rest in the Instant Pot on Keep Warm.

6. When the eggs are cool enough to handle, peel and slice them.

7. To serve, use a slotted spoon to spoon the chorizo into lettuce or cabbage cups. Top with the sliced egg and any of the optional toppings if desired. Or, transfer the chorizo to a serving bowl, put the toppings in individual small bowls, and serve the lettuce or cabbage alongside to create a keto "taco" bar. For a little extra zest, I like a squeeze of lime on top.

If you are one of the unfortunate few who claim to not really care for broccoli, I'm going to challenge you with this creation. You'll become a broccoli lover in no time—really! If you'd prefer, you can also bake this concoction in individual muffin cups or a silicone egg bites mold for a quick grab-and-go breakfast.

BROCCOLI, BACON, AND FETA FRITTATA

MAKES 2 SERVINGS

2   teaspoons avocado oil

4   slices bacon

2   cups broccoli florets, finely chopped

½   teaspoon sea salt

¼   teaspoon ground black pepper

4   large eggs

¼   cup heavy whipping cream

¼   teaspoon ground cumin

¾   cup crumbled feta cheese

1   cup water

MACRONUTRIENTS PER SERVING

CALORIES: 596

FAT: 47 G/426 CALORIES

CARBOHYDRATE: 12 G/29 CALORIES

PROTEIN: 32 G/126 CALORIES

1. Use the avocado oil to grease a stainless steel, Pyrex, or silicone baking dish that fits inside your Instant Pot. If your metal steam rack/trivet does not have handles, make a sling (see Note, page 42).

2. Set the Instant Pot to Sauté. When hot, add the bacon and cook, flipping occasionally, until the bacon is crispy. Remove to a plate.

3. Add the broccoli to the pot and season with ¼ teaspoon of the salt and ⅛ teaspoon of the pepper. Sauté for 3 minutes, then transfer the broccoli to a small bowl. Press Cancel.

4. In a medium bowl, lightly beat together the eggs, cream, cumin, and the remaining ¼ teaspoon salt and ⅛ teaspoon pepper. Crumble the bacon and stir it into the eggs, along with half the feta cheese. Pour the egg mixture into the prepared baking dish. Quickly stir in the broccoli. Sprinkle with the remaining feta cheese. Cover with a metal or silicone lid, or use foil.

5. Wipe out the Instant Pot if desired. Pour in the water and place the steam rack/trivet inside. Arrange the sling over it so the two ends stick up like handles, then lower the baking dish onto the sling and rack.

6. Secure the lid and set the steam release valve to Sealing. Press the Pressure Cook or Manual button and set the cook time to 16 minutes.

7. When the Instant Pot beeps, allow the pressure to release naturally for 5 minutes, then carefully switch the steam release valve to Venting. When fully released, open the lid. Use the sling to carefully remove the hot baking dish. Serve hot or at room temperature.

Smooth, delicious, easy to make—and grain-free! This porridge is completely customizable with toppings and add-ins, so you could have a different porridge every day.

HEMP HEARTS PORRIDGE

MAKES 3 SERVINGS

¼ cup unsweetened shredded or flaked coconut (see Note)

½ cup hemp hearts

3 large eggs

⅓ cup filtered water

1 (13.5-ounce) can full-fat coconut milk

½ teaspoon vanilla extract

1½ teaspoons pumpkin pie spice (see Note)

Scant ¼ teaspoon sea salt

5 to 10 drops of liquid stevia, to taste (optional)

TOPPINGS (OPTIONAL)

Heavy whipping cream

Pecans, walnuts, almonds, hazelnuts

Nut butter, coconut butter, grass-fed butter

More shredded coconut

Fresh berries

1. Set the Instant Pot to Sauté. Add the coconut and hemp to the dry pot insert and cook, stirring frequently, until lightly browned and the hemp starts to smell nutty, 3 minutes.

2. Meanwhile, in a blender, combine the eggs, water, coconut milk, vanilla, pumpkin pie spice, salt, and stevia (if using).

3. Press Cancel on the Instant Pot. Pour the egg mixture into the pot and stir. Secure the lid and set the steam release valve to Sealing. Press the Pressure Cook or Manual button and set the cook time to 1 minute.

4. When the Instant Pot beeps, allow the pressure to release naturally for 5 minutes, then carefully switch the steam release valve to Venting. When fully released, open the lid and give the porridge a good stir. Spoon the porridge into individual serving bowls and add desired toppings.

NOTES

- If you prefer small flakes, pulse them a few times in a food processor.
- If you don't have pumpkin pie spice, you can substitute this combination: 1 teaspoon ground cinnamon, ¼ teaspoon ground ginger, ⅛ teaspoon ground nutmeg, and a pinch of ground cloves.

MACRONUTRIENTS PER SERVING

NO TOPPINGS	WITH 1 TABLESPOON HEAVY WHIPPING CREAM AND 1 TABLESPOON PECANS
CALORIES: 325	CALORIES: 415
FAT: 27 G/243 CALORIES	FAT: 36 G/324 CALORIES
CARBOHYDRATE: 8 G/32 CALORIES	CARBOHYDRATE: 9 G/36 CALORIES
PROTEIN: 16 G/64 CALORIES	PROTEIN: 17 G/68 CALORIES

Who doesn't love rice pudding, but have you ever checked the sugar count on a store-bought product? Ouch! Now you can enjoy a keto-approved substitute that tastes just as satisfying.

BLUEBERRY (CAULIFLOWER) RICE PUDDING

MAKES 4 SERVINGS

2 tablespoons raw cacao butter or coconut oil

4 cups raw cauliflower rice (homemade or store-bought)

1 cup unsweetened almond milk or coconut milk

2 scoops vanilla-flavored protein powder

¼ teaspoon sea salt

½ cup blueberries

Up to 5 drops of liquid stevia (optional, depending on how sweet your protein powder is)

TOPPINGS (OPTIONAL)

Heavy whipping cream, full-fat coconut milk, or coconut cream

Slivered almonds or other chopped nuts

Finely shredded coconut

1. Set the Instant Pot to Sauté and melt the cacao butter.

2. Add the cauliflower rice and stir to coat it with the cacao butter. Add the almond milk, protein powder, salt, blueberries, and stevia (if using) and stir very well to combine.

3. Press Cancel. Secure the lid and set the steam release valve to Sealing. Press the Pressure Cook or Manual button and set the cook time to 3 minutes.

4. When the Instant Pot beeps, allow the pressure to release naturally for 5 minutes, then carefully switch the steam release valve to Venting. When fully released, open the lid and stir the pudding.

5. Spoon the pudding into individual bowls and allow it to cool for a few minutes, then top with the optional toppings of your choosing. Serve warm or at room temperature.

MACRONUTRIENTS PER SERVING

NO TOPPINGS	WITH 1 TABLESPOON EACH OF ALL OPTIONAL TOPPINGS
CALORIES: 147	CALORIES: 276
FAT: 10 G/90 CALORIES	FAT: 22 G/202 CALORIES
CARBOHYDRATE: 9 G/37 CALORIES	CARBOHYDRATE: 12 G/48 CALORIES
PROTEIN: 8 G/30 CALORIES	PROTEIN: 10 G/40 CALORIES

Sardines are one of the healthiest foods on the planet, a treasure trove of omega-3 fatty acids that boost brain health and help regulate inflammation. What better way to start your day than with a dose of healthy fats and veggies?

BIGASS WARM BREAKFAST SALAD WITH SARDINES

MAKES 2 SERVINGS

1	cup water
2	large eggs
1	tablespoon avocado oil
4	slices bacon, cut into small pieces
2	tablespoons minced shallots
1	tablespoon apple cider vinegar
1	(4.4-ounce) can oil-packed sardines
¼	cup fresh parsley leaves
4	cups chopped romaine lettuce
2	cups baby spinach, torn into smaller pieces
¼	teaspoon ground black pepper
1	medium avocado, sliced

MACRONUTRIENTS PER SERVING

CALORIES: 459

FAT: 34 G/306 CALORIES

CARBOHYDRATE: 14 G/56 CALORIES

PROTEIN: 27 G/108 CALORIES

1. Pour the water into the Instant Pot. Place the metal steam rack/trivet inside and place the eggs on top. Secure the lid and set the steam release valve to Sealing. Press the Pressure Cook or Manual button and set the cook time to 10 minutes (refer to the chart on page 30 for adjustments). Meanwhile, prepare a bowl with ice water to cool the eggs.

2. When the Instant Pot beeps, carefully switch the steam release valve to Venting to quick-release the pressure. When fully released, open the lid and use tongs to transfer the eggs to the ice bath. When cool, peel and slice the eggs.

3. Carefully pour the water out of the Instant Pot and wipe it dry. Set the Instant Pot to Sauté and heat the avocado oil. Add the bacon and cook for 3 minutes. Add the shallots and cook until the bacon is crispy, another 1 to 2 minutes. Press Cancel.

4. Deglaze the pot with the vinegar, scraping the bottom with a wooden spoon to loosen any browned bits. Use a fork to break up the sardines and add them, along with their oil, to the pot. Stir in the parsley.

5. Place the lettuce, spinach, and pepper in the pot and mix well to coat the greens with the oil. Divide the mixture between two large serving bowls, scraping any remaining dressing from the pot.

6. Top each salad with half the sliced avocado and 1 sliced egg. Crack some black pepper over the top and serve immediately.

BLUEBERRY
(CAULIFLOWER)
RICE PUDDING
[PAGE 50]

These mushrooms can be assembled the night before and stored in the refrigerator overnight in the cooking pans. In the morning, take it right from the fridge to the Instant Pot and cook as directed. These are delicious with Parmesan or blue cheese melted over the top.

BREAKFAST STUFFED MUSHROOMS

MAKES 2 SERVINGS

12 large white mushrooms, washed, stems removed and reserved

1 tablespoon avocado oil

¼ teaspoon kosher salt

¼ teaspoon ground black pepper

1 tablespoon pork lard or fat of choice

6 ounces sugar-free bulk pork breakfast sausage (see Note)

1 clove garlic, minced

¼ cup full-fat coconut milk, heavy whipping cream, or bone broth (see page 32)

1 cup finely chopped greens of your choosing (spinach, kale, Swiss chard, beet, turnip, etc.)

1 cup water

1. Finely chop the mushroom stems and set aside. Place the mushroom caps stemmed side down in a medium bowl and pour the avocado oil over them. Season with the salt and pepper. Toss gently to coat the mushrooms with oil without breaking them.

2. Set the Instant Pot to Sauté (see Note) and melt the lard. When it is melted, crumble in the sausage and add the chopped mushroom stems. Sauté, stirring occasionally, until only a little pink remains in the pork, 3 to 4 minutes. Add the garlic and sauté until the pork is cooked through.

3. Deglaze the pot with the coconut milk, scraping the bottom with a wooden spoon to loosen any browned bits. Stir in the chopped greens and cook just until they are wilted.

4. Press Cancel. Transfer the pork to a bowl. Taste and adjust the salt and pepper. Wipe or wash out the pot insert.

5. Stuff the pork mixture into the mushrooms. Place the mushrooms stem side up in two stackable stainless steel insert pans, 6 mushrooms per pan. If you have extra pork filling, spoon it over the mushrooms. Stack and secure the lid on the pans.

6. Pour the water into the Instant Pot and lower the stacked pans into the pot. Secure the lid and turn the steam release valve to Sealing. Press the Steam button until High pressure is selected, then set the cook time to 12 minutes.

7. When the Instant Pot beeps, carefully switch the steam release valve to Venting to quick-release the pressure. When fully released, open the lid and use the handle on the insert pans to lift them out (use potholders, it will be hot). Open the insert pans and transfer the mushrooms to serving plates. Serve warm.

NOTES

- If you can't find sugar-free ground breakfast sausage, use ground pork and add 1 teaspoon kosher salt, ½ teaspoon dried sage, and ¼ teaspoon each dried thyme, smoked paprika, and ground black pepper; or you can substitute bulk Italian sausage or a variety of your choosing.
- If you don't have stackable insert pans, you can layer the mushrooms in any heatproof glass or silicone dish that fits in your Instant Pot and cover them tightly with foil. Set the dish on the metal steam rack/trivet after adding water to the pot.
- Steps 2 through 4 can be done in a skillet on the stovetop.

EQUIPMENT

2 (7½-inch-diameter) stackable stainless steel insert pans (see Note)

MACRONUTRIENTS PER SERVING

CALORIES: 476

FAT: 41 G/369 CALORIES

CARBOHYDRATE: 10 G/40 CALORIES

PROTEIN: 10 G/40 CALORIES

BREAKFAST STUFFED
MUSHROOMS [PAGE 54]

There is something Zen-like about carefully spiral-wrapping each asparagus with prosciutto. This is a great way to get kids involved in the kitchen. Serve this at your next brunch to get your guests talking.

EGGS AND PROSCIUTTO-WRAPPED ASPARAGUS SOLDIERS

MAKES 4 SERVINGS

16 thick asparagus spears

4 ounces sliced prosciutto, each slice halved lengthwise

1 cup water

8 large eggs

MACRONUTRIENTS PER SERVING

CALORIES: 203

FAT: 12 G/108 CALORIES

CARBOHYDRATE: 4 G/16 CALORIES

PROTEIN: 19 G/76 CALORIES

1. Prepare the asparagus by cutting off the woody ends and trimming the spears to fit the diameter of your Instant Pot if necessary. Spiral-wrap each spear with prosciutto from bottom to top, allowing a slight overlap.

2. Pour the water into the Instant Pot. Place the metal steam rack/trivet inside. Place the eggs on the rack, standing them upright if possible. Secure the lid and set the steam release valve to Sealing. Press the Pressure Cook or Manual button, adjust the pressure to Low, and set the cook time to 5 minutes. Fill a medium bowl with ice water for the eggs.

3. When the Instant Pot beeps, carefully switch the steam release valve to Venting to quick-release the pressure. When fully released, open the lid. Transfer the eggs to the ice bath.

4. Place the wrapped asparagus on top of the steam rack/trivet. Secure the lid and set the steam release valve to Sealing. Press the Pressure Cook or Manual button and set the cook time to 2 minutes. Meanwhile, transfer the eggs to egg cups (see Note). To remove the tops of the eggshells, gently tap the circumference of one end with the edge of a spoon and lift off the shell and white to expose the creamy yolk.

5. When the Instant Pot beeps, carefully switch the steam release valve to Venting to quick-release the pressure. When fully released, open the lid and transfer the asparagus to serving plates. Serve with the eggs for dipping.

NOTES

- If you prefer crispier prosciutto, after steaming the asparagus in the Instant Pot, heat 2 teaspoons avocado oil in a skillet over medium heat. When it is hot, cook the asparagus spears for 30 to 60 seconds per side, and set on a plate lined with paper towels. You can also do this in the Instant Pot on Sauté.
- If you do not have egg cups, use foil or paper towels to create "nests" in the bottom of your smallest bowls or ramekins to hold the eggs upright. Large shot glasses or cordial glasses might also work, depending on the size of your eggs.

EGGS EN COCOTTE, TWO WAYS

Eggs en cocotte are traditionally baked in a water bath in the oven, so they are perfectly suited to the steamy environment of the Instant Pot. Once you know the basic technique, there are almost endless possibilities for adapting this recipe with your favorite ingredients. The most classic of breakfast combos!

BACON AND CHEESE

MAKES 4 SERVINGS

2 teaspoons avocado oil or melted butter

4 tablespoons diced cooked bacon or ham

6 tablespoons shredded Gruyère or Swiss cheese

4 large eggs

2 tablespoons Cultured Cream (page 184), crème fraîche, or sour cream

1 cup water

Generous pinch of sea salt

Freshly cracked black pepper

MACRONUTRIENTS PER SERVING

CALORIES: 231

FAT: 19 G/173 CALORIES

CARBOHYDRATE: 1 G/4 CALORIES

PROTEIN: 13 G/51 CALORIES

1. Grease the bottom and sides of four 6-ounce ramekins or silicone baking cups with the oil. Place 1 tablespoon each of bacon and shredded cheese into each ramekin. Press it gently into the bottom and create a small divot in the middle.

2. Carefully crack an egg into each ramekin without breaking the yolk. Do not stir. Dab the cultured cream evenly over the eggs and sprinkle each with ½ tablespoon of the remaining cheese. Cover loosely with foil or a silicone lid.

3. Pour the water into the Instant Pot. Place the metal steam rack/trivet inside. Place the ramekins on the rack, stacking them if needed. Secure the lid and set the steam release valve to Sealing. Press the Pressure Cook or Manual button and set the cook time to 8 minutes (see Note).

4. When the Instant Pot beeps, allow the pressure to release naturally for 1 minute, then carefully switch the steam release valve to Venting. When fully released, open the lid. Lift out the hot ramekins with tongs. Season with salt and pepper, and serve hot.

NOTE: Cooked properly, these eggs en cocotte will have creamy but still runny yolks and whites that are just set. Of course, feel free to cook them longer if you want more well-done eggs. You might need to experiment a few times to find the cook time that you prefer.

The inspiration for this recipe comes from the creative folks at Serious Eats (seriouseats.com). Look for domestic crab from Alaska, the Pacific Northwest, California, or Mexico, which gets good scores from the respected marine watchdog group Seafoodwatch.org. Avoid Asian imports, not just for crab but all fish, due to concerns about polluted waters.

CRAB IMPERIAL

2 teaspoons avocado oil or melted butter

6 ounces crabmeat (not imitation!)

⅓ cup avocado oil mayonnaise

2 teaspoons Dijon mustard

1 scallion, white and light-green parts thinly sliced, dark-green tops reserved

¼ teaspoon sweet paprika, plus more for garnish

Hot sauce (optional)

4 large eggs

2 tablespoons heavy whipping cream (or full-fat coconut milk for dairy-free)

Generous pinch of sea salt

Freshly cracked black pepper

1 cup water

MACRONUTRIENTS PER SERVING

CALORIES: 284

FAT: 26 G/234 CALORIES

CARBOHYDRATE: 2 G/8 CALORIES

PROTEIN: 12 G/48 CALORIES

1. Grease the bottom and sides of four 6-ounce ramekins or silicone baking cups with the oil. In a small bowl, combine the crabmeat, mayonnaise, mustard, sliced scallion, and paprika. If desired, add hot sauce to taste. Divide the mixture evenly among the ramekins. Press the mixture into the bottom, creating a divot in the middle of each one.

2. Carefully crack an egg into each ramekin without breaking the yolk. Do not stir. Gently pour ½ tablespoon heavy cream in a circular motion over each egg. Sprinkle with the salt and pepper. Cover loosely with foil or a silicone lid.

3. Pour the water into the Instant Pot. Place the metal steam rack/trivet inside. Place the filled ramekins on the rack, stacking them if needed. Secure the lid and set the steam release valve to Sealing. Press the Pressure Cook or Manual button and set the cook time to 8 minutes (see Note, opposite).

4. When the Instant Pot beeps, allow the pressure to release naturally for 1 minute, then carefully switch the steam release valve to Venting. When fully released, open the lid. Lift out the hot ramekins with tongs. Top each with a dash of paprika. Finely chop the reserved dark-green scallions tops and use it to garnish the eggs.

EGGS EN COCOTTE,
TWO WAYS [PAGE 60]

If someone measured the ORAC (Oxygen Radical Absorbance Capacity—essentially the antioxidant value) of this meal, it would be off the charts! Don't let the long list of ingredients scare you. You'll be pleasantly surprised at how easily this dish comes together. You can even start with frozen seafood if you forget to thaw it—seriously!

SEAFOOD STEW

MAKES 6 SERVINGS

2 tablespoons avocado oil

¼ cup chopped onion

2 stalks celery, sliced

2 cloves garlic, minced

2 small turnips, peeled and cut into ½-inch cubes

2 teaspoons smoked paprika

½ teaspoon celery salt

¼ teaspoon ground white pepper

⅛ teaspoon cayenne pepper (optional)

1 cup diced tomatoes, fresh or canned

1½ pounds cod, fresh or frozen, cut into 1½-inch chunks

½ teaspoon kosher salt

¼ teaspoon ground black pepper

1 cup fish stock or chicken bone broth (see page 32)

1 bay leaf

1 pound shrimp, fresh or frozen, peeled and deveined, tails removed

1. Set the Instant Pot to Sauté and pour in the avocado oil. When hot, add the onion and celery and sauté, stirring frequently, for 2 minutes. Stir in the garlic and sauté for 30 seconds.

2. Stir in the turnips, smoked paprika, celery salt, white pepper, and cayenne (if using) until well coated. Stir in the tomatoes.

3. Season the cod with the salt and black pepper (skip if frozen). Nestle the chunks of cod among the tomatoes. Pour the stock over everything and toss in the bay leaf.

4. Press Cancel. Secure the lid and set the steam release valve to Sealing. Press the Pressure Cook or Manual button and set the cook time to 3 minutes for fresh, 5 minutes for frozen.

5. When the Instant Pot beeps, allow the pressure to release naturally for 5 minutes, then carefully switch the steam release valve to Venting. When fully released, open the lid and stir the contents.

6. Stir the shrimp and the lemon juice into the stew. Secure the lid and allow the shrimp to cook in the hot stew on Keep Warm for 3 minutes for fresh or 5 minutes for frozen. Check to see if the shrimp are opaque. If not, replace the lid and cook for about 2 minutes more.

7. For a creamy stew, gently stir in the cream. After adding the cream, allow the soup to heat back up. (If the soup cools down too much, switch to the Sauté function for a couple minutes.)

8. To serve, discard the bay leaf. Taste and adjust the salt and pepper. Ladle the stew into individual serving bowls. Drizzle each serving with 1 teaspoon olive oil and sprinkle with fresh parsley (if using). Serve with the lemon wedges on the side.

Juice of 1 small lemon

½ cup heavy whipping cream (optional)

2 tablespoons good-quality extra-virgin olive oil

3 tablespoons finely chopped fresh parsley leaves (optional)

1 lemon, cut into 6 wedges, for serving

MACRONUTRIENTS PER SERVING

NO HEAVY WHIPPING CREAM	WITH HEAVY WHIPPING CREAM
CALORIES: 335	CALORIES: 402
FAT: 11 G/99 CALORIES	FAT: 18 G/162 CALORIES
CARBOHYDRATE: 7 G/28 CALORIES	CARBOHYDRATE: 8 G/32 CALORIES
PROTEIN: 52 G/208 CALORIES	PROTEIN: 52 G/208 CALORIES

This recipe is guaranteed to break you out of a chicken slump if you are tired of ordinary preparations. Be sure to get full-fat, not "light," coconut milk for a nice, thick consistency. The daikon radish in this soup stands in for potatoes. You won't be able to tell the difference!

ITALIAN CHICKEN AND SAUSAGE SOUP

MAKES 6 SERVINGS

- 2 teaspoons Italian seasoning (see Note)
- 1 teaspoon kosher salt (reduce or omit if your Italian seasoning blend contains salt)
- ¼ teaspoon ground black pepper
- 2 boneless, skinless chicken breasts
- 3 tablespoons bacon fat or avocado oil
- 12 ounces (¾ pound) fully cooked Italian chicken sausage, mild or spicy, diced
- 1 small bunch Swiss chard, leaves and stems separated, both chopped
- 2 scallions, chopped
- 3 cloves garlic, minced
- 3 cups chicken bone broth (see page 32)
- 1 (13.5-ounce) can full-fat coconut milk

1. In a small bowl, mix together the Italian seasoning, salt, and pepper. Use this mixture to season the chicken all over. Allow the chicken to sit at room temperature while you move on to the next steps.

2. Set the Instant Pot to Sauté and add 1½ tablespoons of the fat. When it is hot, add the diced sausage and cook, stirring frequently, until it is browned, about 3 minutes. Use a slotted spoon to transfer the sausage to a bowl.

3. Add the remaining 1½ tablespoons fat to the pot. Add the chopped chard stems only (not the leaves), the scallions, and garlic and sauté until the garlic is browned and fragrant, 1 to 2 minutes.

4. Pour in 1 cup of the chicken broth and use a wooden spoon to scrape the bottom of the pot to release any browned bits. Place the chicken breasts in the pot.

5. Press Cancel. Secure the lid and turn the steam release valve to Sealing. Press the Pressure Cook or Manual button and set the cook time to 10 minutes.

6. When the Instant Pot beeps, allow the pressure to release naturally for 5 minutes, then carefully switch the steam release valve to Venting. When fully released, open the lid. Use tongs to transfer the chicken to a plate.

7. Add the remaining 2 cups chicken broth and the coconut milk to the pot. Stir in the chard leaves, daikon, and cooked sausage along with any reserved juices from the bowl.

8. Press Cancel. Secure the lid and set the steam release valve to Sealing. Press the Pressure Cook or Manual button and set the cook time to 3 minutes.

9. While that cooks, let the chicken rest for a few minutes, then chop it into bite-size pieces.

10. When the Instant Pot beeps, allow the pressure to release naturally for 5 minutes, then carefully switch the steam release valve to Venting. Open the lid and stir the chopped chicken into the soup. Allow the soup to sit for a minute or two to warm up the chicken. Stir in the fresh parsley, ladle into individual serving bowls, and serve hot.

NOTE: You can substitute 1 teaspoon dried oregano, ½ teaspoon dried basil, ¼ teaspoon dried thyme, and ¼ teaspoon marjoram (optional) for the Italian seasoning.

1 large daikon radish, peeled and cut into ½-inch cubes

½ cup finely chopped fresh parsley leaves

MACRONUTRIENTS PER SERVING

CALORIES: 309
FAT: 19 G/173 CALORIES
CARBOHYDRATE: 6 G/26 CALORIES
PROTEIN: 27 G/109 CALORIES

ITALIAN CHICKEN
AND SAUSAGE SOUP
[PAGE 68]

It's no secret that keto folks are crazy for avocado, but if you want a break from guacamole, throw this delicious, nutritious, highly satisfying Mexican and South American soup into the mix.

AVOCADO SOUP

MAKES 4 SERVINGS

2 avocados

1 small tomatillo, fresh or canned, quartered

2 cups chicken bone broth (see page 32) or vegetable stock

2 tablespoons avocado oil

1 tablespoon butter or ghee (or more avocado oil)

2 tablespoons finely minced onion

1 clove garlic, minced

½ serrano chile, seeded and ribs removed, minced, plus thin slices for garnish

¼ teaspoon sea salt

Pinch of ground white pepper

½ cup heavy whipping cream or full-fat coconut milk

Fresh cilantro sprigs, for garnish

Queso fresco or Homemade Ricotta (page 187; optional)

1. Scoop the avocado flesh into a blender or food processor. Add the tomatillo and bone broth and puree until smooth. Set aside.

2. Set the Instant Pot to Sauté and add the avocado oil and butter. When the butter has stopped foaming, add the onion and garlic and sauté, stirring frequently, until just softened, about 1 minute. Add the serrano chile and sauté 1 minute more. Press Cancel.

3. Pour the pureed avocado mixture into the pot, add the salt and pepper, and stir to combine. Secure the lid and set the steam release valve to Sealing. Press the Pressure Cook or Manual button and set the cook time to 5 minutes.

4. When the Instant Pot beeps, carefully switch the steam release valve to Venting to quick-release the pressure. Open the lid and stir in the cream.

5. Serve hot topped with thin slices of serrano chile, cilantro sprigs, and crumbled queso fresco or ricotta (if using).

MACRONUTRIENTS PER SERVING

NO CHEESE	WITH CHEESE
CALORIES: 323	CALORIES: 366
FAT: 31 G/281 CALORIES	FAT: 35 G/312 CALORIES
CARBOHYDRATE: 9 G/36 CALORIES	CARBOHYDRATE: 9 G/37 CALORIES
PROTEIN: 9 G/36 CALORIES	PROTEIN: 8 G/30 CALORIES

If you've ever had a bland restaurant appetizer of the same name, get ready to discover what real living is all about! Sip it slowly to enjoy the unique blend of ingredients.

CREAMY SPINACH ARTICHOKE SOUP

MAKES 4 SERVINGS

3	tablespoons salted butter
8	ounces cremini mushrooms, sliced
1	small jar (6 ounces) artichoke hearts packed in water or olive oil
4	ounces full-fat cream cheese
1	tablespoon Dijon mustard
1	teaspoon dried sage
1	teaspoon dried thyme
½	teaspoon garlic powder
½	teaspoon kosher salt
¼	teaspoon ground black pepper
¼	teaspoon red pepper flakes (optional)
2	cups chicken bone broth (see page 32)
1	cup filtered water
2	cups roughly chopped baby spinach
½	cup heavy whipping cream
½	cup grated Parmesan

MACRONUTRIENTS PER SERVING

CALORIES: 288

FAT: 22 G/198 CALORIES

CARBOHYDRATE: 12 G/48 CALORIES

PROTEIN: 14 G/56 CALORIES

1. Set the Instant Pot to Sauté and add the butter. When it starts to foam, add the mushrooms and sauté, stirring frequently, for about 8 minutes.

2. Meanwhile, drain the artichoke hearts. If the ends are tough, trim and discard them. Roughly chop the artichokes and set aside.

3. When the mushrooms are soft, add the cream cheese to the pot and stir until it is melted. Stir in the mustard, sage, thyme, garlic powder, salt, black pepper, and pepper flakes (if using). Stir in the bone broth, water, and artichoke hearts.

4. Press Cancel. Secure the lid and set the steam release valve to Sealing. Press the Pressure Cook or Manual button and set the cook time to 5 minutes.

5. When the Instant Pot beeps, allow the pressure to release naturally for 5 minutes, then carefully switch the steam release valve to Venting. When fully released, open the lid.

6. Stir in the baby spinach and replace the lid. Do not change the settings, simply allow the spinach to cook for 2 minutes in the soup on Keep Warm. Open the lid and stir.

7. Optional but highly recommended: Use an immersion blender to blend the soup to your liking.

8. Stir in the cream. Taste and adjust the salt and pepper.

9. To serve, ladle the soup into individual serving bowls and sprinkle each with 2 tablespoons of Parmesan. Serve hot.

AVOCADO SOUP
[PAGE 72]

This popular Vietnamese soup is pronounced "fuh," with an upward inflection. Traditional cooking methods call for a broth that has been simmered for several hours, but cooking under pressure allows for a full-flavored broth in a fraction of the time. The high cartilage content of the oxtails lends a velvety mouthfeel. The heat from the broth cooks the raw beef slices to a perfect medium-rare in the time it takes to add your toppings.

BEEF PHO (PHO BO)

MAKES 4 SERVINGS

FOR THE BROTH

- 1½   pounds oxtails
- ½   pound beef brisket or chuck roast
- 1   cinnamon stick
- 5   whole cloves
- ⅛   teaspoon ground coriander
- 2   star anise pods
- ½   medium onion, thickly sliced

  2-inch piece fresh ginger, thickly sliced and bruised

- 10   cups filtered water
- ½   medium Fuji apple (see Note), peeled and cut into chunks
- 2   teaspoons sea salt
- 2   teaspoons fish sauce, or more to taste

  Keto-friendly sweetener (optional)

1. For the broth: Rinse the oxtails and brisket well under cold running water. Place the oxtails and brisket in a large stockpot and cover with water. Bring the water to a rolling boil over high heat, then reduce to a low boil and cook for 15 minutes. You will see a beige colored raft of foam form on the surface of the water. Remove the pot from the heat, discard the water, and rinse the oxtails and brisket with warm water when they are cool enough to handle. Set the beef aside.

2. Set the Instant Pot to Sauté. Once heated, place the cinnamon, cloves, coriander, and star anise in the bottom of the dry pot insert and toast for 2 to 3 minutes, stirring constantly. Add the onion and ginger and continue to stir for an additional minute or two. The aromatics will begin to smell very fragrant during this time, and it is desirable if they begin to char slightly. Press Cancel.

3. Carefully pour in the water, then add the oxtails, brisket, apple, and salt. Secure the lid and set the steam release valve to Sealing. Press the Pressure Cook or Manual button and set the cook time to 15 minutes.

4. Meanwhile, place the sirloin in the freezer for 20 to 30 minutes (this makes it easier to slice later). Place the optional toppings in small bowls to prepare for serving later.

WITH MUNG BEAN SPROUTS
CALORIES: 356
FAT: 12 G/108 CALORIES
CARBOHYDRATE: 11 G/42 CALORIES
PROTEIN: 46 G/185 CALORIES

5. When the Instant Pot beeps, allow the pressure to release naturally for 20 minutes, then carefully switch the steam release valve to Venting. When fully released, open the lid. Very carefully strain the hot broth from the pot through a fine-mesh sieve. Set the brisket aside and discard the ginger, onion, apple, and spices. Leftover bones and cartilaginous bone caps from the oxtails can be saved and used again later to make bone broth. Season the strained broth with fish sauce to taste. Adjust the flavor by adding sweetener to taste, if desired.

6. Remove the sirloin from the freezer and slice thinly across the grain. Likewise slice the cooked brisket. Divide the spiralized zucchini noodles evenly among four large soup bowls. Arrange slices of both raw and cooked beef atop the zucchini noodles, along with slices of red onion and scallion. Gently pour a generous serving of piping hot broth into each bowl directly over top of the raw beef slices and zucchini noodles. Serve immediately with the optional toppings on the side for diners to add themselves, along with lime wedges.

NOTE: Keto folks might be tempted to omit the apple from this recipe, but don't! You discard it after cooking, and it adds minimal carbs per serving.

TO ASSEMBLE

6 ounces sirloin steak

2 large zucchini, spiralized into thin noodles

¼ red onion, thinly sliced

2 scallions, thinly sliced on a diagonal

Lime wedges, for serving

TOPPINGS (OPTIONAL)

1 cup mung bean sprouts or other sprouted greens

Few sprigs each of fresh Thai basil, cilantro, and/or mint

Thai chiles or jalapeños, thinly sliced

BEEF PHO (PHO BO)
[PAGE 76]

This keto-friendly version of the classic potato leek soup is hearty and perfect for cold weather. Leeks, garlic, and onions are good sources of prebiotic inulin fiber.

BACON CAULIFLOWER LEEK SOUP

MAKES 6 SERVINGS

1   leek

6   slices bacon

½   medium yellow onion, sliced

4   cloves garlic, minced

3   cups chicken bone broth (see page 32)

1   cup filtered water

1   large head cauliflower, roughly chopped into florets

1   teaspoon kosher salt

1   teaspoon ground black pepper

⅔   cup shredded sharp cheddar cheese

½   cup heavy whipping cream

MACRONUTRIENTS PER SERVING

CALORIES: 217

FAT: 15 G/132 CALORIES

CARBOHYDRATE: 12 G/48 CALORIES

PROTEIN: 11 G/44 CALORIES

1. Prepare the leek by removing and discarding the dark green end and roots. Slice the leek in half lengthwise and rinse it under running water to remove any sandy soil from between the layers. Once clean, cut it crosswise into ½-inch-thick slices. If desired, reserve a couple tablespoons of chopped leek for garnishing the finished soup.

2. Set the Instant Pot to Sauté. When heated, place the bacon in a single layer on the bottom of the pot and cook until crispy. Remove the bacon slices to a plate. When it is cool enough to handle, crumble it.

3. Add the leek and onion to the bacon fat remaining in the pot. Sauté until fragrant and the onion begins to caramelize, 3 to 5 minutes. Add the garlic and sauté 30 seconds more.

4. Deglaze the pot with 1 cup of the bone broth, scraping the bottom with a wooden spoon to loosen any browned bits. Stir in the remaining 2 cups bone broth, the water, cauliflower florets, salt, pepper, and three-quarters of the crumbled bacon.

5. Press Cancel. Secure the lid and set the steam release valve to Sealing. Press the Pressure Cook or Manual button and set the cook time for 3 minutes.

6. When the Instant Pot beeps, carefully switch the steam release valve to Venting to quick-release the pressure. When fully released, open the lid. Stir in ½ cup of the cheddar and the cream. Use an immersion blender to puree the soup until smooth (see Note). Taste and season with salt and pepper as needed.

7. Ladle into serving bowls and top with a twist of freshly cracked black pepper. Garnish with the remaining cheddar and crumbled bacon (and leek slices if desired).

NOTE: A handheld potato masher, blender, or food processor may also be used to puree the soup. If using a blender or food processor, use caution and work in small batches—heated liquids are prone to splattering.

Crazy title, crazy delicious. Make sure to eat this right away while the melted cheese is still smokin'!

BACON CHEESEBURGER SOUP

MAKES 6 SERVINGS

1   tablespoon bacon fat or avocado oil

4   slices bacon, cut into small pieces

½   cup diced onion

2   stalks celery, thinly sliced

1½   pounds grass-fed ground beef

1   tablespoon dried oregano

1   tablespoon dried parsley flakes

1   tablespoon dried basil

1   teaspoon kosher salt

½   teaspoon ground black pepper

4   cups bone broth (see page 32)

1   large daikon radish, peeled and cut into ½-inch cubes

½   cup sour cream

2½   cups shredded sharp cheddar cheese

12   slices dill pickle, for garnish (optional)

MACRONUTRIENTS PER SERVING

CALORIES: 557

FAT: 40 G/360 CALORIES

CARBOHYDRATE: 9 G/34 CALORIES

PROTEIN: 40 G/158 CALORIES

1. Set the Instant Pot to Sauté and melt the bacon fat. When the fat is hot, add the chopped bacon and sauté for 3 minutes. Add the onion and celery and sauté, stirring frequently, until the bacon is cooked and the onion is just soft, another 3 to 5 minutes.

2. Use your hands to crumble the ground beef into the pot. Crush the dried oregano between your palms and add it to the meat. Add the parsley, basil, salt, and black pepper and stir everything in the pot well, breaking up the meat as you stir. Sauté for 3 minutes, continuing to break up any big chunks of meat with a wooden spoon or meat chopper.

3. Deglaze the pot with about ½ cup of the bone broth, scraping the bottom with a wooden spoon to loosen any browned bits. Stir in the rest of the bone broth and the daikon radish.

4. Press Cancel. Secure the lid and set the steam release valve to Sealing. Select the Soup function. Set the pressure to High and the cook time to 5 minutes.

5. When the Instant Pot beeps, allow the pressure to release naturally for 10 minutes, then carefully switch the steam release valve to Venting. When fully released, open the lid.

6. Stir in the sour cream and 2 cups of the cheddar. Allow the soup to cook a few minutes more on the Keep Warm setting, stirring occasionally. Taste and adjust the salt and pepper.

7. Ladle the soup into individual serving bowls. Top each serving with a generous tablespoon of cheddar and 2 pickle slices (if using). Enjoy hot.

Rutabagas—also known as swedes or neeps—are a cross between a cabbage and a turnip, making them a member of the brassica family. This rich soup combines kale, mushrooms, and rutabaga for a filling, antioxidant-rich meal.

CHICKEN SAUSAGE, KALE, AND RUTABAGA SOUP

MAKES 6 SERVINGS

2 tablespoons extra-virgin olive oil

12 ounces fully cooked chicken sausage, sliced

½ medium onion, chopped

2 cloves garlic, minced

5 cups chicken bone broth (see page 32) or stock

3 cups roughly chopped curly kale leaves

8 ounces mushrooms, sliced

½ cup peeled and diced rutabaga

2 tablespoons apple cider vinegar

½ teaspoon red pepper flakes

1 teaspoon sea salt

¼ teaspoon ground black pepper

1 cup heavy whipping cream or full-fat coconut milk

1. Set the Instant Pot to Sauté. When hot, add the oil and swirl to coat the bottom. Add the sliced sausage and cook, stirring occasionally, until browned, 3 to 4 minutes. Add the onion and garlic and sauté until the onions become translucent and the garlic turns golden, an additional 3 minutes. Press Cancel.

2. Stir in the broth, kale, mushrooms, rutabaga, vinegar, pepper flakes, salt, and black pepper. Secure the lid and set the steam release valve to Sealing. Press the Pressure Cook or Manual button and set the cook time to 8 minutes.

3. When the Instant Pot beeps, carefully switch the steam release valve to Venting. When fully released, open the lid and stir in the cream. Allow the soup to rest for 2 to 3 minutes on Keep Warm before ladling into serving bowls and serving hot.

MACRONUTRIENTS PER SERVING

CALORIES: 330

FAT: 26 G/236 CALORIES

CARBOHYDRATE: 8 G/32 CALORIES

PROTEIN: 17 G/66 CALORIES

Who knew pork and pumpkin went together? Well, they do in this recipe! Try adding the avocado for a colorful presentation and a perfect match for the other two leading ingredients.

SPICY PORK AND PUMPKIN SOUP

MAKES 4 SERVINGS

1½ pounds boneless pork shoulder (butt), cut into 1½-inch cubes

1 teaspoon ground cumin

½ teaspoon garlic powder

½ teaspoon sea salt

¼ teaspoon ground black pepper

2 tablespoons pork lard or fat of choice

1 cup unsweetened pumpkin puree, homemade (page 35) or canned

1 cup filtered water

2 cups chicken bone broth (see page 32)

½ cup chopped onion

1 (4.5-ounce) can chopped green chilies

1 fresh jalapeño, seeded and ribs removed, minced

⅛ teaspoon cayenne pepper (optional)

4 cups chopped greens of choice (spinach, kale, Swiss chard, beet, turnip, etc.)

1. In a large bowl, toss the pork with the cumin, garlic powder, salt, and pepper. Allow it to sit for 20 minutes.

2. Set the Instant Pot to Sauté and heat the pork lard. When it is hot, add the pork shoulder and let brown for 3 to 4 minutes without disturbing, then stir and brown another 3 to 4 minutes. Meanwhile, in a bowl, whisk together the pumpkin puree and water.

3. Add the bone broth to the pot and use a wooden spoon to scrape the bottom of the pot to loosen any browned bits. Stir in the pumpkin mixture, onion, chilies, jalapeño, and cayenne (if using).

4. Secure the lid and set the steam release valve to Sealing. Press the Pressure Cook or Manual button and set the cook time to 30 minutes.

5. When the Instant Pot beeps, allow the pressure to release naturally for 10 minutes, then carefully switch the steam release valve to Venting. When fully released, open the lid and stir the contents. Taste the broth and adjust the salt and black pepper. Stir in the greens and cook on Keep Warm just until wilted.

6. Ladle the soup into individual serving bowls. If using the optional toppings, top each bowl with 1 tablespoon sour cream, one-quarter of the cubed avocado, and a sprinkling of cilantro. Cut a slit in the flesh of the lime wedges and affix 2 to the edge of each bowl. Serve hot.

MACRONUTRIENTS PER SERVING

NO TOPPINGS		WITH ALL OPTIONAL TOPPINGS
CALORIES: 590		CALORIES: 678
FAT: 38 G/342 CALORIES		FAT: 46 G/414 CALORIES
CARBOHYDRATE: 12 G/48 CALORIES		CARBOHYDRATE: 16 G/66 CALORIES
PROTEIN: 47 G/188 CALORIES		PROTEIN: 48 G/194 CALORIES

TOPPINGS (OPTIONAL)

4 tablespoons sour cream

1 small avocado, cubed

¼ cup fresh cilantro leaves

1 lime, cut into 8 wedges, for serving

VEGGIES
& SIDES

_____

92

96

101

103

106

109

111

Cauliflower mash goes with just about any entree you can imagine. Add herbs to change the flavor profile, top with cheese, or keep it super simple with just butter or olive oil and salt. The parsnip here changes the final flavor and texture to be more like mashed potatoes.

EASY MASHED CAULIFLOWER

MAKES 4 SERVINGS

1 cup water

1 large head cauliflower, cut into florets (about 6 cups)

1 small parsnip, peeled and cubed

1 tablespoon butter or ghee (or olive oil for dairy-free)

1 to 2 tablespoons sour cream (or coconut cream for dairy-free, or just omit)

¼ teaspoon garlic powder

¼ teaspoon sea salt

¼ teaspoon ground black pepper

2 tablespoons minced fresh chives

MACRONUTRIENTS PER SERVING

CALORIES: 91

FAT: 5 G/44 CALORIES

CARBOHYDRATE: 10 G/42 CALORIES

PROTEIN: 4 G/16 CALORIES

1. Pour the water into the Instant Pot. Place a metal steaming basket inside. Place the cauliflower and parsnip in the basket. Secure the lid and set the steam release valve to Sealing. Press the Pressure Cook or Manual button and set the cook time to 5 minutes.

2. When the Instant Pot beeps, carefully switch the steam release valve to Venting to quick-release the pressure. When fully released, open the lid. Leave the Instant Pot set to Keep Warm. Use a slotted spoon to transfer the vegetables to a bowl. Carefully remove the steaming basket, pour out the water, and wipe the pot insert dry with a clean kitchen towel.

3. Return the vegetables to the pot (which is still on Keep Warm). Add the butter, 1 tablespoon of the sour cream, the garlic powder, salt, and pepper. Use an immersion blender to blend until very smooth, or leave some texture if you prefer. Taste and adjust the salt and pepper, and stir in the additional sour cream if desired.

4. Stir in the chives (don't blend). Serve hot or warm.

Pressure-cooking asparagus can be tricky because it can go from crisp to mushy in practically no time. Make sure you stay within earshot of your Instant Pot so you can release the pressure as soon as the cooking is done. Cooking it as described here yields the same results as blanching, a common cooking technique for asparagus, but in less time than it takes to boil a pot of water.

GARLICKY ASPARAGUS

MAKES 4 SERVINGS

1 large bunch asparagus, woody ends cut off (medium-thick spears if possible)

1 cup water

2 tablespoons salted butter

2 large cloves garlic, minced

2 teaspoons fresh lemon juice (from ½ lemon)

¾ cup finely shredded Parmesan cheese (optional)

Salt

MACRONUTRIENTS PER SERVING

NO CHEESE
CALORIES: 70
FAT: 6 G/53 CALORIES
CARBOHYDRATE: 4 G/16 CALORIES
PROTEIN: 2 G/8 CALORIES

WITH CHEESE
CALORIES: 154
FAT: 11 G/102 CALORIES
CARBOHYDRATE: 4 G/19 CALORIES
PROTEIN: 10 G/38 CALORIES

1. Cut the asparagus spears on a diagonal into 3 equal pieces, or trim the whole spears to fit your Instant Pot.

2. Pour the water into the Instant Pot. Place a metal steaming basket inside. Place the asparagus in the basket. Secure the lid and set the steam release valve to Sealing. Press the Pressure Cook or Manual button and set the cook time to 1 minute for tender (for softer, increase to 2 minutes; for crisp, decrease to 0). While it cooks, prepare a bowl with ice water.

3. When the Instant Pot beeps, carefully switch the steam release valve to Venting to quick-release the pressure. When fully released, open the lid and use tongs to transfer the asparagus to the ice bath. Let it sit for a minute, then drain and place the asparagus on a clean kitchen towel and pat dry.

4. Carefully remove the pot insert. Remove the steaming basket, drain the water, and wipe the pot insert dry.

5. Return the pot insert to the Instant Pot and press the Sauté button. Put the butter in the pot. When it has melted and starts to foam, add the garlic and sauté, stirring, for 1 minute.

6. Return the asparagus to the pot and stir well to coat it with the garlic-butter mixture. Add the lemon juice. Sauté until it reaches the desired doneness, about 1 minute more.

7. Transfer the asparagus to a serving bowl and stir in the Parmesan. Taste the asparagus and add salt to taste. Serve warm.

**SPAGHETTI SQUASH
WITH RED SAUCE AND
PINE NUTS** [PAGE 92]

This isn't your mama's boxed noodles and jarred spaghetti sauce replete with added sugars. You have my permission to pass on the anchovies, but they are in there for a reason! Don't miss out on the wonderful umami they offer. If you are an anchovy lover, you can even use the olive oil from the can or jar of anchovies to drizzle over the finished dish.

SPAGHETTI SQUASH WITH RED SAUCE AND PINE NUTS

MAKES 4 SERVINGS

½ cup pine nuts (pignoli)

1 medium spaghetti squash

¼ teaspoon sea salt

¼ teaspoon ground black pepper

2 cups Red Sauce (recipe follows)

4 to 8 anchovy fillets packed in olive oil, to taste, chopped

¼ cup fresh basil chiffonade (see Note)

2 tablespoons good-quality extra-virgin olive oil

MACRONUTRIENTS PER SERVING

CALORIES: 320

FAT: 25 G/229 CALORIES

CARBOHYDRATE: 17 G/68 CALORIES

PROTEIN: 8 G/32 CALORIES

1. Set the Instant Pot to Sauté. When hot, toast the pine nuts in the dry pot insert, stirring constantly, until they are lightly browned, 1 to 2 minutes. Press Cancel. Transfer the pine nuts to a bowl and set aside.

2. Prepare and cook the spaghetti squash as directed on page 34.

3. Carefully drain the water from the pot insert and wipe it dry. Return the squash noodles to the pot and select the Keep Warm function. Season with the salt and pepper. Add the red sauce and stir to coat the noodles. If the red sauce is cold, you can switch to Sauté to heat it up more quickly, but stir it frequently so the bottom does not burn.

4. As soon as the red sauce is warm, hit Cancel. Stir in the anchovies and basil, then transfer the mixture to a serving dish. Drizzle with the olive oil and sprinkle with the toasted pine nuts. Serve warm.

NOTE: It sounds fancy, but chiffonade simply means to cut the basil into thin ribbons. To do this, stack the basil leaves on top of each other, then starting from the side roll the stack into a tight cigar. Use a sharp knife to cut the cigar crosswise into very thin slices about 1/16 inch wide.

Perfect for pairing with spaghetti squash. Make a double batch and freeze the extra to have an easy replacement for sugary store-bought marinara sauces.

RED SAUCE

2 tablespoons extra-virgin olive oil

1 teaspoon oil reserved from the can or jar of anchovies (see Note)

2 anchovy fillets packed in olive oil

2 cloves garlic, minced

½ medium onion, diced

1 tablespoon dried oregano

½ to 1 teaspoon red pepper flakes, to taste

1 (28-ounce) can crushed San Marzano tomatoes

¼ cup minced fresh basil

Sea salt and ground black pepper

MACRONUTRIENTS PER ½ CUP

CALORIES: 98

FAT: 6 G/54 CALORIES

CARBOHYDRATE: 7 G/28 CALORIES

PROTEIN: 2 G/10 CALORIES

1. Set the Instant Pot to Sauté. Once heated, add the olive oil and anchovy oil and swirl to coat the bottom of the pot. Add the anchovies and cook until soft, breaking apart the fillets with a wooden spoon, about 2 minutes. Add the garlic and onion and sauté, stirring frequently, until the onion becomes translucent, 3 to 4 minutes. Crush the oregano between your palms and add it to the pot along with the pepper flakes. Cook for an additional minute to awaken the aromatic oils. Press Cancel.

2. Stir in the tomatoes. Secure the lid and set the steam release valve to Sealing. Press the Pressure Cook or Manual button and set the cook time to 45 minutes.

3. When the Instant Pot beeps, carefully switch the steam release valve to Venting to quick-release the pressure. When fully released, open the lid and stir in the fresh basil. Season with salt and pepper to taste.

4. The sauce can be served immediately or transferred to a jar and refrigerated. Chilled leftover sauce freezes well and can be stored for up to 3 months in the freezer.

NOTE: The extra teaspoon of the anchovy-infused oil intensifies the savory umami notes of this sauce. You can substitute an additional teaspoon of olive oil instead.

Before you eat it, take a picture of this beauty to post to social media (see page 183). The vibrant colors put any sugary parfait to shame!

SAVORY BEET AND BASIL PARFAIT

SERVES 4 AS A SIDE DISH OR SNACK

1   cup water

1   large beet, unpeeled, greens removed

3   tablespoons plus 2 teaspoons good-quality extra-virgin olive oil

1   teaspoon balsamic vinegar

½   cup fresh basil leaves

½   cup chopped walnuts

⅛   teaspoon sea salt

1   teaspoon fresh lemon juice

1   cup yogurt (see Note)

1   teaspoon grated lemon zest (optional), for garnish

MACRONUTRIENTS PER SERVING

CALORIES: 300

FAT: 28 G/256 CALORIES

CARBOHYDRATE: 9 G/35 CALORIES

PROTEIN: 6 G/22 CALORIES

1. Pour the water into the Instant Pot. Place the metal steam rack/trivet inside. Place the beet on the rack. Secure the lid and set the steam release valve to Sealing. Press the Pressure Cook or Manual button and set the cook time to 20 minutes.

2. When the Instant Pot beeps, carefully switch the steam release valve to Venting to quick-release the pressure. When fully released, open the lid. Use tongs to transfer the beet to a bowl.

3. When cool enough to handle, hold the beet under running water and use your hand to rub off the skin, which will slide right off. Finely dice the beet—this is a messy job!

4. Measure out 1 cup of beets (save any extra to use as a topping for your next Bigass Salad). In a small bowl, stir together the diced beets, 2 teaspoons of the olive oil, and the balsamic vinegar. Set aside.

5. In a small food processor, combine the basil, walnuts, salt, and lemon juice and pulse until the basil is roughly chopped. Scrape down the sides of the food processor and add the remaining 3 tablespoons of olive oil. Pulse until the basil is finely chopped and the ingredients are incorporated. Do not overprocess, you want it to have some texture.

6. If using the combination of yogurt and ricotta (see Note), stir them together. Assemble the parfaits in four small bowls or 4-ounce mason jars in the following manner:

a. Stir the beets, then place 2 tablespoons of beets in the bottom of each bowl.

b. Place a spoonful of the walnut pesto on top and gently spread to cover the beets.

c. Spoon 2 tablespoons of yogurt (or yogurt/ricotta) over the walnut mixture.

d. Repeat these steps to form a second layer of beets, walnuts, and yogurt.

7. If desired, garnish with the lemon zest. Serve immediately or transfer to the refrigerator until ready to serve.

NOTE: Use Homemade Dairy Yogurt (page 180) or Homemade Coconut Yogurt (page 182) or a combination of ½ cup yogurt mixed with ½ cup Homemade Ricotta (page 187). Because beets are a moderation food on a keto diet, these portions are purposefully small. If you are eating a higher carbohydrate profile, feel free to double the portion sizes.

This dish makes a fantastic accompaniment to a nice juicy steak on any given night, but also think about doubling the recipe and serving it at your next holiday meal. Since it doesn't require the already crowded stove or oven to prepare, it's perfect for gatherings. It looks nice on the holiday table, too!

BUTTERY HERBED MUSHROOMS

MAKES 4 SERVINGS

4   tablespoons unsalted butter or ghee

3   cloves garlic, minced

4   cups small cremini or white mushrooms (see Note), stems removed

½   cup loosely packed fresh parsley leaves

4   sprigs fresh oregano, leaves picked

4   sprigs fresh thyme, leaves picked

1   cup bone broth (see page 32) or vegetable broth

1   teaspoon kosher salt

½   teaspoon ground black pepper

¼   teaspoon dried marjoram (optional)

1. Set the Instant Pot to Sauté. Add the butter and when it starts to foam add the garlic and mushrooms. Cook, stirring occasionally, for 5 minutes.

2. Meanwhile, set aside 2 tablespoons of the parsley. Place the remaining parsley, oregano leaves, and thyme leaves on a cutting board. Run a sharp knife several times through the herbs to chop them together. Push them into a pile and roughly chop them once more.

3. Add the chopped herbs to the mushrooms and stir well. In a small bowl, whisk together the broth, salt, pepper, and marjoram (if using). Pour the broth mixture over the mushrooms. Press Cancel. Secure the lid and turn the steam release valve to Sealing. Press the Pressure Cook or Manual button and set the cook time to 5 minutes.

4. When the Instant Pot beeps, carefully switch the steam release valve to Venting to quick-release the pressure. When fully released, open the lid. Use a slotted spoon to transfer the mushrooms to a serving bowl.

5. Press Cancel and then Sauté. Taste the cooking liquid and adjust the salt and pepper. Bring the liquid to a boil and cook, stirring frequently, for 3 to 5 minutes to slightly thicken the liquid. Press Cancel.

6. Very carefully pour or ladle the hot liquid over the mushrooms. Garnish with the reserved parsley. Serve hot or at room temperature.

NOTE: If possible, choose mushrooms that are about the same size. If you can only find bigger mushrooms, cut them in half, or even quarters if they are quite large.

MACRONUTRIENTS PER SERVING

CALORIES: 140

FAT: 12 G/108 CALORIES

CARBOHYDRATE: 7 G/28 CALORIES

PROTEIN: 4 G/16 CALORIES

INDIAN-STYLE
OKRA [PAGE 101]

Now you can never again say you don't know what to do with a rutabaga! Rutabaga is a great option for restocking glycogen after strenuous exercise. Keto folks can enjoy this root veggie in moderation while being mindful of the carbohydrates. In this recipe, the glycemic load is moderated by the inclusion of nutritious fats.

GARLIC MASHED RUTABAGA

MAKES 4 SERVINGS

2 tablespoons avocado oil

2 cloves garlic, smashed

2 cups peeled and cubed rutabaga (about 10 ounces)

1 cup filtered water, bone broth (see page 32), or stock

1½ teaspoons sea salt

¼ cup heavy whipping cream or full-fat coconut milk

2 tablespoons finely chopped fresh parsley leaves, for garnish

MACRONUTRIENTS PER SERVING

CALORIES: 162

FAT: 13 G/117 CALORIES

CARBOHYDRATE: 9 G/36 CALORIES

PROTEIN: 3 G/12 CALORIES

1. Set the Instant Pot to Sauté and heat the oil. When hot, add the garlic and cook for 1 minute, stirring. Press Cancel.

2. Add the rutabaga, water, and salt. Secure the lid and set the steam release valve to Sealing. Press the Pressure Cook or Manual button and set the cook time to 6 minutes.

3. When the Instant Pot beeps, carefully switch the steam release valve to Venting. When fully released, open the lid. Use a slotted spoon to transfer the rutabaga and garlic to a large bowl. Blend with a hand mixer (preferred) or immersion blender until smooth. As you blend, slowly adding the cream 1 tablespoon at a time until the rutabaga reaches the desired consistency. Serve immediately with the parsley sprinkled over top.

This recipe is an adaptation of bhindi masala, or okra curry. Okra is a great source of fiber and vitamin K, but some folks have a hard time getting past its admittedly slimy texture. If you're on the fence about okra, try this dish and see if the interesting flavor profiles win you over. I'm betting yes!

INDIAN-STYLE OKRA

MAKES 6 SERVINGS

1 pound young okra (see Note)

4 tablespoons ghee or avocado oil

½ teaspoon cumin seeds

¼ teaspoon ground turmeric

Pinch of ground cinnamon

½ medium onion, diced

2 cloves garlic, minced

2 teaspoons minced fresh ginger

1 serrano chile, seeded and ribs removed, minced

1 small tomato, diced

½ teaspoon sea salt

¼ teaspoon cayenne pepper (optional)

1 cup vegetable stock or filtered water

MACRONUTRIENTS PER SERVING

CALORIES: 114

FAT: 9 G/81 CALORIES

CARBOHYDRATE: 9 G/36 CALORIES

PROTEIN: 2 G/8 CALORIES

1. Rinse and thoroughly dry the okra. Slice it on a diagonal into slices ½ to ¾ inch thick, discarding the stems.

2. Set the Instant Pot to Sauté. Once hot, add the ghee and heat until melted. Stir in the cumin seeds, turmeric, and cinnamon and cook until they are fragrant, about 1 minute. This may cause the cumin seeds to jump and pop. Add the onion and cook, stirring frequently, until soft and translucent, about 3 minutes. Add the garlic, ginger, and serrano chile and sauté for an additional minute. Press Cancel.

3. Stir in the tomato, okra, salt, cayenne (if using), and stock. Secure the lid and set the steam release valve to Sealing. Press the Pressure Cook or Manual button and set the cook time to 2 minutes.

4. When the Instant Pot beeps, carefully switch the steam release valve to Venting to quick-release the pressure. When fully released, open the lid. Stir gently and allow the okra to rest on the Keep Warm setting for a few minutes before serving.

NOTE: If you have misgivings about the texture of cooked okra, select young or "baby" okra for this dish. Young okra produces less mucilage than the larger, older pods.

Collard greens with ham is a staple dish in the southern US. The tender greens and "pot liquor"—the cooking liquid that results from braising the ham and greens—are both comforting and addictive. The problem is that the traditional dish takes hours to prepare on the stovetop. Maybe if the word gets out about how easy collard greens are to make in the Instant Pot, they'll become as hip as their cousin, kale.

BRAISED COLLARD GREENS AND HAM

MAKES 4 SERVINGS

2 tablespoons avocado oil or fat of choice

1 small onion, chopped

2 cloves garlic, smashed

½ teaspoon red pepper flakes

¼ teaspoon sea salt

2 cups chicken bone broth (see page 32) or stock

1 pound smoked ham hocks

1 pound collard greens, chopped

1 teaspoon apple cider vinegar, or more to taste

MACRONUTRIENTS PER SERVING

CALORIES: 339

FAT: 22 G/193 CALORIES

CARBOHYDRATE: 9 G/36 CALORIES

PROTEIN: 30 G/118 CALORIES

1. Set the Instant Pot to Sauté. When hot, add the oil and onion. Cook, stirring frequently, until the onion is soft and translucent, about 3 minutes. Add the garlic, pepper flakes, and salt. Sauté 1 minute more. Press Cancel.

2. Pour in the bone broth. Set the ham hock at the bottom of the pot. Add the greens to the pot, along with the vinegar. Secure the lid and set the steam release valve to Sealing. Press the Pressure Cook or Manual button and set the cook time to 60 minutes.

3. When the Instant Pot beeps, carefully switch the steam release valve to Venting to quick-release the pressure. When fully released, open the lid. Use tongs to remove the ham hock to a cutting board. Shred the meat off the bones with two forks. Mix the shredded meat back into the greens in the pot. Taste and adjust salt.

4. Serve the greens warm, topped with a generous ladle of pot liquor.

This dish is wonderful as a side for baked or steamed fish. Or, for a meat-free meal, whip up a batch of Easy Mashed Cauliflower (page 88) and serve this over the top like a deconstructed cottage pie with Moroccan flavors!

MOROCCAN-SPICED ZUCCHINI

MAKES 4 SERVINGS

2   tablespoons avocado oil

½   medium onion, diced

1   clove garlic, minced

¼   teaspoon cayenne pepper

¼   teaspoon ground coriander

¼   teaspoon ground cumin

¼   teaspoon ground ginger

     Pinch of ground cinnamon

1   Roma (plum) tomato, diced

2   medium zucchini, cut into 1-inch pieces

½   tablespoon fresh lemon juice

¼   cup bone broth (see page 32) or vegetable stock

MACRONUTRIENTS PER SERVING

CALORIES: 92

FAT: 7 G/67 CALORIES

CARBOHYDRATE: 6 G/23 CALORIES

PROTEIN: 2 G/8 CALORIES

1. Set the Instant Pot to Sauté. When hot, add the oil. Add the onion and sauté, stirring frequently, until translucent, about 2 minutes. Add the garlic, cayenne, coriander, cumin, ginger, and cinnamon and cook until fragrant, about 1 minute. Stir in the tomato and zucchini and cook 2 minutes longer.

2. Press Cancel. Add the lemon juice and broth. Secure the lid and set the steam release valve to Sealing. Press the Pressure Cook or Manual button, adjust the pressure to Low, and set the cook time to 1 minute.

3. When the Instant Pot beeps, carefully switch the steam release valve to Venting to quick-release the pressure. When fully released, open the lid. Stir and serve warm.

I don't do a lot of baking with nut flours, but I make an exception for this one. It has a subtle sweetness that complements the rosemary and hint of lemon. Serve this alongside soup or chili for dunking, or top with a schmear of Cultured Butter (page 186).

OLIVE OIL ROSEMARY BREAD

MAKES 8 SERVINGS

1 cup extra-virgin olive oil, plus 1 tablespoon for greasing the pan

4 large eggs

1¼ cups almond flour

¼ cup ground flaxseed meal

1 teaspoon baking powder

1 tablespoon Swerve Confectioner sweetener or liquid stevia (optional)

1 tablespoon finely ground fresh rosemary

¼ teaspoon kosher salt

1 tablespoon grated lemon zest

1 tablespoon fresh lemon juice

5 drops liquid stevia

1½ cups water

MACRONUTRIENTS PER SERVING

CALORIES: 409

FAT: 41 G/369 CALORIES

CARBOHYDRATE: 6 G/26 CALORIES

PROTEIN: 8 G/30 CALORIES

1. Use 1 tablespoon of olive oil to grease the bottom and sides of a 6- to 7-inch stainless steel, Pyrex, or silicone baking pan that fits in your Instant Pot.

2. In a medium bowl, whisk together the remaining 1 cup of olive oil and the eggs. In a second bowl, combine the almond flour, flax meal, baking powder, Swerve (if using), rosemary, and salt. Pour the wet ingredients into the dry and stir well to combine. Add in the lemon zest, lemon juice, and stevia, and stir until just incorporated.

3. Pour the batter into the prepared baking pan and tap the pan on your counter a few times to settle the batter. Cover the pan loosely with a lid or foil.

4. Pour the water into the Instant Pot and place the metal steam rack/trivet inside. If your rack does not have handles, make a sling (see Note, page 42). Arrange the sling over the trivet so the two ends stick up like handles, then lower the baking dish onto the sling and rack. Secure the lid and set the steam release valve to Sealing. Press the Pressure Cook or Manual button and set the cook time to 45 minutes.

5. When the Instant Pot beeps, allow the pressure to release naturally for 10 minutes, then carefully switch the steam release valve to Venting. When fully released, open the lid. Use the sling to carefully remove the baking dish. Allow the bread to cool in the pan for 10 minutes, then carefully invert it onto a serving plate. Serve warm or at room temperature.

ARTICHOKES WITH ROASTED GARLIC BUTTER

MAKES 4 SERVINGS

4 medium artichokes (see Note)

1 lemon, halved, plus 1 lemon, cut into wedges, for serving

1 cup water

8 tablespoons Roasted Garlic Compound Butter (page 177) or 8 tablespoons unsalted butter plus 2 cloves garlic, grated

MACRONUTRIENTS PER SERVING

CALORIES: 272
FAT: 23 G/209 CALORIES
CARBOHYDRATE: 15 G/59 CALORIES
PROTEIN: 5 G/18 CALORIES

NOTE: "Medium" artichokes weigh about ¼ pound and are approximately the size of softballs. If you are using larger artichokes, you will need to adjust the cooking time accordingly. Start by adding 3 to 5 minutes of cooking time. You can always reseal the Instant Pot and add more time if needed.

1. Prepare the artichokes by trimming the stems flush with the bottoms. Peel away any browned outer leaves. Chop off the tops of the artichokes (about one-quarter of the way down). Using kitchen shears, snip off the thorny tips of the remaining leaves. Rinse the artichokes under running water and shake off excess water. Rub the cut edges of the artichokes with the cut half of the lemon to help slow them from browning.

2. Pour the water into the Instant Pot. Place the metal steam rack/trivet or steamer basket inside. Set the artichokes upright on the rack, stacking them if necessary. Secure the lid and turn the steam release valve to Sealing. Press the Pressure Cook or Manual button and set the cook time to 10 minutes.

3. When the Instant Pot beeps, allow the pressure to release naturally for 10 minutes, then carefully switch the steam release valve to Venting.

4. Meanwhile, if using the already-made compound butter, melt it in a small saucepan over low heat. If making fresh garlic butter, gently melt the butter in a small saucepan over medium heat, stir in the grated garlic, and simmer for 1 minute. Remove either garlic butter from the heat.

5. When the pressure is fully released, open the lid. Use tongs to carefully remove the artichokes to serving plates. Serve the artichokes with lemon wedges and individual dishes of melted garlic butter for dipping.

Brussels sprouts and the Instant Pot are a match made in heaven. Pancetta is a close cousin of bacon, which of course pairs wonderfully with Brussels sprouts. If you've never tried blue cheese on your sprouts, you're in for a treat.

BRUSSELS SPROUTS WITH PANCETTA AND NUTS

½ pound pancetta, diced

1 clove garlic, chopped

1 pound (about 4 cups) Brussels sprouts, ends trimmed, halved if large

1 tablespoon balsamic vinegar

½ teaspoon ground black pepper

½ cup filtered water or bone broth (see page 32)

⅔ cup crumbled blue cheese (omit for dairy-free)

½ cup walnuts or pecans, chopped

MACRONUTRIENTS PER SERVING

CALORIES: 432

FAT: 34 G/309 CALORIES

CARBOHYDRATE: 14 G/55 CALORIES

PROTEIN: 18 G/72 CALORIES

1. Set the Instant Pot to Sauté. When hot, add the pancetta and sauté for 2 minutes. Add the garlic and sauté until the pancetta is browned, another 1 to 2 minutes. Add the Brussels sprouts, vinegar, and pepper and stir well to combine. Pour in the water.

2. Press Cancel. Secure the lid and set the steam release valve to Sealing. Press the Pressure Cook or Manual button and set the cook time to 3 minutes. (Add another 1 or 2 minutes if you prefer very soft Brussels sprouts.)

3. When the Instant Pot beeps, carefully switch the steam release valve to Venting to quick-release the pressure. When fully released, open the lid and stir the Brussels sprouts.

4. Use a slotted spoon to transfer the Brussels sprouts and pancetta to a serving bowl. Add the blue cheese and half the nuts to the Brussels sprouts, and stir quickly until thoroughly mixed. Sprinkle with the rest of the nuts and serve hot.

CAULIFLOWER MAC AND CHEESE

MAKES 6 SERVINGS

1 cup water

1 large cauliflower, chopped into bite-size florets

1 cup heavy whipping cream

½ cup sour cream

1 cup shredded Gruyère or mozzarella cheese

2½ cups shredded sharp cheddar cheese

1 teaspoon ground mustard

1 teaspoon ground turmeric

Sea salt

Pinch of cayenne pepper (optional)

MACRONUTRIENTS PER SERVING

CALORIES: 371

FAT: 31 G/279 CALORIES

CARBOHYDRATE: 8 G/32 CALORIES

PROTEIN: 18 G/72 CALORIES

1. Pour the water into the Instant Pot. Place a metal steaming basket inside. Put the cauliflower florets in the basket. Secure the lid and set the steam release valve to Sealing. Press the Pressure Cook or Manual button and set the cook time to 3 minutes. When the Instant Pot beeps, carefully switch the steam release valve to Venting to quick-release the pressure. When fully released, open the lid.

2. Meanwhile, prepare the cheese sauce. In a large skillet, gently bring the cream to a simmer over medium to medium-low heat. Whisk in the sour cream until smooth, then gradually whisk in the Gruyère and 2 cups of the cheddar until melted. Stir in the ground mustard and turmeric. Taste and adjust the salt.

3. Remove the cauliflower from the pot and toss it in the cheese sauce to coat. Serve warm, topped with the remaining cheddar and a sprinkling of cayenne (if using).

Braising is a delicious way to prepare cabbage, and perfectly suited for the Instant Pot. Prepared this way, the subtle sweetness of the cabbage really shines.

BRAISED GINGER CABBAGE

MAKES 6 SERVINGS

1 tablespoon avocado oil

1 tablespoon butter or ghee (or more avocado oil)

½ medium onion, diced

1 medium bell pepper (any color), diced

1 teaspoon sea salt

½ teaspoon ground black pepper

1 clove garlic, minced

1-inch piece fresh ginger, grated

1 pound green or red cabbage, cored, leaves chopped

½ cup bone broth (see page 32) or vegetable broth

1. Set the Instant Pot to Sauté and heat the oil and butter together. When the butter has stopped foaming, add the onion, bell pepper, salt, and black pepper. Sauté, stirring frequently, until just softened, about 3 minutes. Add the garlic and ginger and cook 1 minute longer. Add the cabbage and stir to combine. Pour in the broth.

2. Secure the lid and set the steam release valve to Sealing. Press the Pressure Cook or Manual button and set the cook time to 2 minutes.

3. When the Instant Pot beeps, carefully switch the steam release valve to Venting to quick-release the pressure. When fully released, open the lid. Stir the cabbage and transfer it to a serving dish. Serve warm.

MACRONUTRIENTS PER SERVING

CALORIES: 73

FAT: 5 G/45 CALORIES

CARBOHYDRATE: 7 G/28 CALORIES

PROTEIN: 2 G/8 CALORIES

A traditional Lenten dish, this gumbo can be made with or without meat. Virtually any leafy green can be used in this recipe. Good options include kale, Swiss chard, collard greens, mustard greens, cabbage, bok choy, and spinach, as well as edible root vegetable tops such as beet greens. This is a thrifty and delicious way to make use of a crisper full of random greens.

LOUISIANA GREEN GUMBO

MAKES 8 SERVINGS

- 2 tablespoons avocado oil
- 1 medium onion, chopped
- 2 stalks celery, leaves included, chopped
- 1 small green bell pepper, diced
- 3 cloves garlic, smashed
- 2 cups bone broth (see page 32), stock, or filtered water
- 6 ounces okra (see Note), chopped
- 1 pound andouille sausage, sliced (optional)
- 1 tablespoon sea salt
- 1 tablespoon Cajun or Creole seasoning (no sugar added)
- 3 bay leaves
- ½ teaspoon dried oregano
- ½ teaspoon dried thyme
- 1 tablespoon fresh lemon juice
- ¾ to 1 pound assorted chopped greens, stems and tough center ribs removed

1. Set the Instant Pot to Sauté and heat the avocado oil. Add the onion, celery, and bell pepper and cook for 5 minutes, stirring often. Add the garlic and cook until golden and fragrant, an additional 1 to 2 minutes. Press Cancel.

2. Add the broth, okra, andouille (if using), salt, Cajun seasoning, bay leaves, oregano, thyme, and lemon juice. Stir well to combine. Add the greens one large handful at a time and stir until wilted. Secure the lid and set the steam release valve to Sealing. Press the Pressure Cook or Manual button and set the cook time for 20 minutes.

3. When the Instant Pot beeps, carefully switch the steam release valve to Venting to quick-release the pressure. When fully released, open the lid. Remove and discard the bay leaves. Taste and adjust the salt. Ladle into soup bowls to serve.

NOTE: If you are not a fan of okra, you can omit the okra and substitute more greens. It won't be gumbo exactly—it will be delicious braised greens instead!

MACRONUTRIENTS PER SERVING

NO SAUSAGE	WITH SAUSAGE
CALORIES: 71	CALORIES: 309
FAT: 4 G/34 CALORIES	FAT: 19 G/173 CALORIES
CARBOHYDRATE: 8 G/32 CALORIES	CARBOHYDRATE: 6 G/26 CALORIES
PROTEIN: 3 G/12 CALORIES	PROTEIN: 27 G/109 CALORIES

ENTREES

118

122

124

126

129

131

136

138

142

144

147

152

155

158

Pulled pork is simply the best if you like to prep food for the week or if you are feeding a crowd (or just a family with a couple teenagers!). It is delicious on its own, and it makes an excellent base for lettuce-wrapped tacos, soups, stews, omelets, and hashes. Check out the recipe for Pulled Pork Burrito Bowls (page 122) and Creamy Pork and Mushroom Stew (page 124) for two tasty ways to use the leftovers.

PULLED PORK

MAKES ABOUT SIX 5-OUNCE SERVINGS

¼ cup plus 2 tablespoons avocado oil

Juice of 2 limes

1 tablespoon kosher salt

1 tablespoon ground cumin

1 teaspoon ground coriander

1 teaspoon garlic powder

¼ teaspoon ground cinnamon

Approximately 3½ pounds boneless pork shoulder (butt), large fat deposits trimmed, cut into 4 pieces

1 cup bone broth (see page 32) or filtered water

MACRONUTRIENTS PER 5-OUNCE SERVING

CALORIES: 532

FAT: 43 G/386 CALORIES

CARBOHYDRATE: 2 G/9 CALORIES

PROTEIN: 33 G/132 CALORIES

1. In a large glass bowl, mix together ¼ cup of the avocado oil, the lime juice, and all the seasonings. Add the pork and toss to coat. Marinate at room temperature for 30 minutes, or cover and refrigerate for up to 8 hours.

2. When you are ready to cook, set the Instant Pot to Sauté and add the remaining 2 tablespoons avocado oil. When the oil is hot, add two pieces of the pork and brown for 3 minutes. Flip and brown 3 minutes on the second side. Remove the browned pork to a plate and repeat for the other two pieces of pork. Reserve the marinade.

3. Pour the broth into the pot and use a wooden spoon to scrape the bottom of the pot to loosen any browned bits. Return all the pork to the pot along with any juices that collected on the plate. Pour the reserved marinade over the pork.

4. Press Cancel. Secure the lid and set the steam release valve to Sealing. Press the Pressure Cook or Manual button and set the cook time to 90 minutes.

5. When the Instant Pot beeps, allow the pressure to release naturally for 10 minutes, then carefully switch the steam release valve to Venting. When fully released, open the lid. Use tongs to carefully remove one piece of pork at a time to a cutting board. Use two forks to shred the meat. Place the shredded meat in a large bowl. If desired, scoop ¼ cup of the cooking liquid and stir it into the shredded pork, adding more liquid ¼ cup at a time until the pork is as moist as you prefer.

BONUS STEP

Spread the shredded pork out on a heavy rimmed baking sheet or broiler pan. Drizzle with more avocado oil. Position a rack about 4 inches below the heat and heat the broiler to low. Place the pan under the broiler until the meat is browned and some pieces have become crispy. Watch it carefully. Toss with tongs before serving.

This rustic dish is an excellent one to serve to company. By using the Instant Pot, the cooking time is reduced by hours. Tell folks to eat the delicious marrow, too!

OSSO BUCO

4   bone-in beef shanks

    Sea salt

2   tablespoons avocado oil

1   medium onion, diced

1   small carrot, diced

1   medium stalk celery, diced

4   cloves garlic, smashed

1   tablespoon tomato paste

½   cup dry white wine

2   sprigs fresh thyme

1   sprig fresh rosemary

1   cup bone broth (see page 32) or stock

3   Roma (plum) tomatoes, diced

FOR THE GREMOLATA

½   cup loosely packed parsley leaves

1   clove garlic, crushed

    Grated zest of 2 lemons (preferably organic)

MACRONUTRIENTS PER SERVING WITH
4 OUNCES BEEF SHANK MEAT

CALORIES: 232

FAT: 9 G/78 CALORIES

CARBOHYDRATE: 7 G/27 CALORIES

PROTEIN: 26 G/104 CALORIES

1. Season the shanks all over with salt. Set the Instant Pot to Sauté and add the oil. When the oil shimmers, add 2 of the shanks and sear 3 to 4 minutes per side. Remove the shanks to a bowl and repeat with the other 2 shanks. Set aside.

2. Add the onion, carrot, and celery to the pot and cook until softened, about 5 minutes. Add the garlic and tomato paste and cook 1 minute more, stirring frequently. Deglaze the pot with the wine, scraping the bottom with a wooden spoon to loosen any browned bits. Allow the wine to come to a boil. Press Cancel.

3. Add the thyme, rosemary, broth, and shanks (along with any accumulated juices from the bowl), then add the tomatoes on top of the shanks. Secure the lid and set the steam release valve to Sealing. Press the Pressure Cook or Manual button and set the cook time to 40 minutes.

4. Meanwhile, for the gremolata: In a small food processor, combine the parsley, garlic, and lemon zest and pulse until the parsley is very finely chopped. Refrigerate until ready to use.

5. When the Instant Pot beeps, allow the pressure to release naturally for 20 minutes, then carefully switch the steam release valve to Venting. When fully released, open the lid.

6. To serve, transfer the shanks to large, shallow serving bowl. Ladle the braising sauce over the top and sprinkle with the gremolata.

PULLED PORK BURRITO
BOWLS [PAGE 122]

One of the cool, less well known features of the Instant Pot is that it can be used to heat up leftovers, which is great for people who prefer not to microwave food. The results from the Instant Pot are better, too! The food retains its moisture and heats evenly. There are several options for reheating pulled pork, but these two are my preferred.

PULLED PORK BURRITO BOWLS

MAKES 4 SERVINGS

1½ tablespoons pork lard or fat of choice

1 small green bell pepper, sliced

1 small red bell pepper, sliced

½ medium onion, sliced

1 clove garlic, chopped

¼ teaspoon ground cumin

¼ teaspoon kosher salt

1 pound leftover Pulled Pork (page 116)

½ cup chicken bone broth (see page 32)

¼ to 1 cup filtered water

FOR THE BURRITOS

6 cups chopped lettuce or spring mix

6 cups shredded green cabbage or store-bought slaw mix

⅓ cup sour cream

¼ cup salsa of choice

½ cup prepared guacamole

¼ cup minced fresh cilantro leaves

OPTION 1

1. Set the Instant Pot to Sauté and melt the lard. Add the bell peppers and onion and sauté, stirring frequently, for 2 minutes. Add the garlic, cumin, and salt and stir well to combine. Press Cancel.

2. Stir in the pulled pork and pour in the broth. (If your meat is very dry, add ¼ to ½ cup water.) Secure the lid and set the steam release valve to Sealing. Press the Pressure Cook or Manual button and set the cook time to 1 minute.

3. While the pork heats, begin to assemble the burritos: Divide the lettuce and cabbage equally among four large salad bowls. If desired, in a small bowl, stir together the sour cream and salsa and set aside.

4. When the Instant Pot beeps, carefully switch the steam release valve to Venting to quick-release the pressure. When fully released, open the lid. Use tongs to stir the meat and vegetables.

5. Use the tongs to place a heaping serving of the pulled pork and vegetables on top of each salad. Top each with 2 tablespoons guacamole. If you mixed the salsa and sour cream together, drizzle about 2 tablespoons of the mixture over each salad. Otherwise, simply place a dollop of each on the salad. Finally, sprinkle with fresh cilantro and serve.

OPTION 2

1. Place the leftover pulled pork in a Pyrex, stainless steel, or silicone baking dish that fits inside your Instant Pot. Pour the ½ cup broth over the pork unless you saved it in its own cooking liquid and it is already quite moist. Cover the baking dish with a silicone lid or a metal lid from your pots and pans. Otherwise, use foil.

2. Pour 1 cup of water into the Instant Pot. If your metal steam rack/trivet does not have handles, make a sling (see Note, page 42). Place the steam rack/trivet inside and arrange the sling over it so the two ends stick up like handles, then lower the dish onto the sling and rack.

3. Secure the lid and select the Steam function. Set the cook time to 5 minutes.

4. While the pork reheats, in a medium skillet, melt the lard over medium heat. Add the bell peppers and onion and sauté, stirring frequently, for 3 minutes. Stir in the garlic, cumin, and salt and sauté 1 to 2 minutes more. Remove the skillet from the heat.

5. Begin to assemble the burritos: Divide the lettuce and cabbage equally among four large salad bowls. Place a serving of the sautéed peppers and onions on each. If desired, in a small bowl, stir together the sour cream and salsa and set aside.

6. When the Instant Pot beeps, carefully switch the steam release valve to Venting to quick-release the pressure. When fully released, open the lid. Use the sling to carefully remove the pork.

7. Stir the pulled pork, then use tongs to place a heaping serving on top of each salad. Top each with 2 tablespoons guacamole. If you mixed the salsa and sour cream together, drizzle about 2 tablespoons of the mixture over each salad. Otherwise, simply place a dollop of each on the salad. Finally, sprinkle with fresh cilantro and serve.

MACRONUTRIENTS PER SERVING

CALORIES: 508

FAT: 37 G/333 CALORIES

CARBOHYDRATE: 20 G/79 CALORIES

PROTEIN: 27 G/107 CALORIES

Another delicious way to use leftover pulled pork (or leftover shredded or rotisserie chicken). The dish comes together in mere minutes, making it a perfect option for a midweek meal.

CREAMY PORK AND MUSHROOM STEW

MAKES 4 SERVINGS

2   tablespoons avocado oil

2   cloves garlic, minced

¾   cup bone broth (see page 32)

½   teaspoon dried crushed rosemary

¼   teaspoon dried thyme

10   ounces cremini mushrooms, sliced or quartered

1   large yellow squash, halved lengthwise and cut crosswise into ½-inch slices

3   cups leftover Pulled Pork (page 116)

1   cup Cultured Cream (page 184), Homemade Dairy Yogurt (page 180), crème fraîche, or full-fat Greek yogurt

4   cups baby spinach

Salt

1. Set the Instant Pot to Sauté and heat the avocado oil. Add the garlic and sauté 1 minute. Slowly pour in the broth. Stir in the rosemary, thyme, mushrooms, and squash. Mix in the shredded pork.

2. Press Cancel. Secure the lid and set the steam release valve to Sealing. Press the Pressure Cook or Manual button and set the cook time to 5 minutes.

3. When the Instant Pot beeps, allow the pressure to release naturally for 5 minutes, then switch the steam release valve to Venting. When fully released, open the lid.

4. Press Cancel and then Sauté. Stir in the cultured cream and spinach. Set to Keep Warm and cook just until the spinach is wilted. Taste-test and add salt if needed. Ladle into individual serving bowls and enjoy hot.

MACRONUTRIENTS PER SERVING

CALORIES: 853

FAT: 73 G/653 CALORIES

CARBOHYDRATE: 11 G/45 CALORIES

PROTEIN: 41 G/162 CALORIES

This is an original recipe from the co-author on *The Keto Reset Diet* and *Primal Endurance*, Brad Kearns, who really knows how to be creative in the kitchen. Cooking a whole chicken is yet another thing the Instant Pot can do. You couldn't run to the store and grab a rotisserie chicken this fast, and it wouldn't be nearly as flavorful anyway.

LEMON GARLIC TOMATO WALNUT CHICKEN

MAKES 6 SERVINGS

- 1 whole pasture-raised chicken (3 to 4 pounds)
- ½ cup avocado oil
- 1 small onion, chopped
- 1½ tablespoons finely chopped sun-dried tomatoes
- 2 teaspoons Italian seasoning (see Note, page 69)
- 8 cloves garlic, chopped
- ⅓ cup finely chopped walnuts
- 1 lemon, quartered, plus lemon slices for garnish
- 1 teaspoon kosher salt (reduce or omit if your Italian seasoning blend contains salt)
- 1 cup filtered water or bone broth (see page 32)

MACRONUTRIENTS PER SERVING
BASED ON A 3-POUND CHICKEN

CALORIES: 481

FAT: 29 G/258 CALORIES

CARBOHYDRATE: 5 G/20 CALORIES

PROTEIN: 49 G/198 CALORIES

1. Rinse the chicken inside and out and pat dry.

2. In a blender or small food processor, combine ⅓ cup of the avocado oil, the onion, sun-dried tomatoes, Italian seasoning, and garlic. Blend until smooth. Add the walnuts and pulse a few times.

3. Squeeze the lemon juice over the chicken, then place the spent lemon rinds inside the cavity of the chicken. Spread the walnut mixture all over the surface of the bird (top and bottom), place the chicken in a shallow baking dish or bowl, and marinate in the refrigerator for at least 2 hours.

4. Remove the chicken from the refrigerator and allow to sit at room temperature for 20 to 30 minutes. Scrape off the chunky marinade from the outside of the chicken, but do not discard. Season the outside of the chicken with salt.

5. Set the Instant Pot to Sauté and pour in the remaining avocado oil. When the oil starts to smoke, carefully place the chicken breast side down in the hot oil. Allow it to brown for about 3 minutes, the use your largest spatula and a pair of tongs to carefully lift it out of the oil and flip it. Let the chicken brown for 3 minutes on the second side.

6. If you do not want the chicken cooking in liquid, carefully lift it out of the Instant Pot, place the metal steam rack/

trivit inside, and place the chicken on the rack. Otherwise, simply pour the water around the chicken. Spoon the reserved marinade back over the surface of the chicken.

7. Press Cancel. Secure the lid and set the steam release valve to Sealing. Press the Pressure Cook or Manual button and set the cook time to 25 minutes for a smaller bird or up to 35 minutes for a larger bird (the rule of thumb is 8 minutes per pound).

8. When the Instant Pot beeps, allow the pressure to release naturally, 10 to 15 minutes. When fully released, open the lid and remove the chicken to a serving platter to rest for a few minutes. Garnish with lemon slices and serve.

Research confirms that mussels are among the most nutrient-dense foods on the planet—a favorite of humans for over 20,000 years! They offer some of the highest concentrations of omega-3 fatty acids (highest of any shellfish), along with key minerals like iron, manganese, phosphorus, potassium, selenium, and zinc. I don't know about you, but until recently I'd only eaten mussels in a restaurant because I guessed—incorrectly—that they might be hard to make. Now you can flex your mussel muscles with this simple and delicious recipe.

GARLICKY MUSSELS

MAKES 2 SERVINGS

4 tablespoons salted butter

1 large shallot, minced

4 cloves garlic, minced

2 pounds mussels, scrubbed and debearded (see Note)

1 cup chicken bone broth (see page 32)

   Juice of 1 large lemon

3 tablespoons chopped fresh parsley leaves

MACRONUTRIENTS PER SERVING

CALORIES: 383

FAT: 27 G/239 CALORIES

CARBOHYDRATE: 13 G/52 CALORIES

PROTEIN: 24 G/95 CALORIES

1. Set the Instant Pot to Sauté and melt the butter. When the butter is beginning to foam, add the shallot and garlic and sauté until fragrant and lightly browned, 1 to 2 minutes.

2. Place the mussels in the pot. Pour the broth and lemon juice over the mussels.

3. Press Cancel. Secure the lid and set the steam release valve to Sealing. Press the Pressure Cook or Manual button and set the cook time to 3 minutes.

4. When the Instant Pot beeps, carefully switch the steam release valve to Venting to quick-release the pressure. When fully released, open the lid. Discard any mussels that did not open during cooking.

5. Carefully transfer the mussels to a serving bowl. Pour any remaining liquid from the pot over the mussels and sprinkle with the parsley. Serve and enjoy.

NOTE: To prepare mussels, wash them well and debeard them. Rinse them in a colander and scrub them with a scrub brush under running water. If any of the mussels have a beard—a hairy bit that sticks out between the shells near the hinge—grab it with your fingers and pull it off. Mussels are only safe to cook if they are shut (which means they are still alive). Test open mussels by tapping them on the counter. If they close, they are safe to cook.

This keto-friendly twist on classic comfort food is sure to please the whole family. You can assemble the meatballs in advance and refrigerate them in an airtight container between layers of waxed paper until ready to use.

SWEDISH MEATBALLS

MAKES 4 SERVINGS

2 large eggs

1½ pounds grass-fed ground beef

3 tablespoons onion, grated or very finely minced

¾ teaspoon dried parsley flakes

½ teaspoon ground allspice

½ teaspoon ground nutmeg

½ teaspoon garlic powder

1 teaspoon sea salt

½ teaspoon ground black pepper

2 tablespoons avocado oil

1 cup beef broth

½ cup full-fat coconut milk, heavy whipping cream, Cultured Cream (page 184), or crème fraîche

1 teaspoon Dijon mustard

1 tablespoon arrowroot flour

MACRONUTRIENTS PER SERVING

CALORIES: 603

FAT: 42 G/382 CALORIES

CARBOHYDRATE: 4 G/17 CALORIES

PROTEIN: 48 G/191 CALORIES

1. In a large mixing bowl, lightly beat the eggs. Add the ground beef, onion, parsley, allspice, nutmeg, garlic powder, salt, and pepper. With your hands, mix everything together until it is thoroughly combined.

2. Pour the avocado oil into the Instant Pot and swirl the pot to coat the bottom. Form the ground beef mixture into meatballs slightly larger than a golf ball (about 2 tablespoons of meat per meatball). Place the meatballs in the Instant Pot. If they do not fit in a single layer, create a second layer on top.

3. Pour the beef broth over the meatballs. Secure the lid and set the steam release valve to Sealing. Press the Manual button and adjust the cook time to 6 minutes.

4. When the Instant Pot beeps, allow the pressure to release naturally for 10 minutes, then carefully switch the steam release valve to Venting to quick-release the pressure. When fully released, open the lid. Use a slotted spoon to remove the meatballs to a bowl.

5. Whisk the coconut milk and Dijon mustard into the cooking liquid in the pot. Press Cancel, then Sauté. Allow the mixture to come to a boil. Carefully ladle about ¼ cup of the hot liquid into a bowl. Whisk the arrowroot flour into this liquid until smooth, then pour the slurry back into the pot, whisking constantly. Allow the mixture to boil for 1 to 2 minutes until thickened. Taste and adjust the salt and pepper.

6. Add the meatballs back to the pot and stir to cover them with the sauce. Cook another 2 minutes. Serve hot.

Brisket can be dry and tough if not prepared correctly, but it's hard to mess up in a pressure cooker. You don't even have to brown it if you don't want to, you can just throw it in and cook it. Grab a big brisket from your local farmer, cook this on Sunday, and eat brisket all week.

BRISKET WITH CABBAGE AND HORSERADISH SAUCE

MAKES 8 SERVINGS

FOR THE BRISKET

- 3 pounds beef brisket
- 1½ teaspoons kosher salt
- 1 teaspoon ground black pepper
- 1 tablespoon bacon fat or avocado oil (optional)
- ½ small onion, cut into ½-inch slices
- 2 cloves garlic, smashed
- ¾ cup filtered water

FOR THE HORSERADISH SAUCE

- ¼ cup sour cream
- ¼ cup Cultured Cream (page 184) or crème fraîche (or more sour cream)
- 1 to 3 tablespoons prepared horseradish, to taste
- 1 tablespoon Dijon mustard, preferably whole-grain
- 2 teaspoons fresh lemon juice
- ¼ teaspoon sea salt
- ¼ teaspoon ground black pepper

1. Trim any large deposits of fat from the brisket (do not go overboard trying to get all the fat off). Cut the brisket across the grain into 4 pieces. Season the top and bottom with the salt and pepper.

2. Optional but recommended: Set the Instant Pot to Sauté and melt the bacon fat, swirling to coat the bottom of the pot. Place the brisket in the hot fat and brown on the first side for 3 minutes. Flip with tongs and brown 3 minutes more on the other side. You will probably need to do this in two batches. Remove the brisket to a plate and press Cancel.

3. Scatter the onion slices on the bottom of the pot insert. Place the brisket on top of the onions in a single layer if possible, but overlap or stack them if necessary rather than squeezing them in. Toss in the garlic and pour in the water.

4. Secure the lid and turn the steam release valve to Sealing. Press Meat/Stew and make sure the High pressure light is illuminated. (If not, press the Meat/Stew button until High pressure is selected.) Set the cook time to 60 minutes.

5. Meanwhile, for the horseradish sauce: In a small bowl, stir together the sour cream, cultured cream, horseradish, mustard, lemon juice, salt, and pepper. Refrigerate until serving time.

(recipe continues)

6. When the Instant Pot beeps, allow the pressure to release naturally for 10 minutes, then carefully switch the steam release valve to Venting. When fully released, open the lid. Check the meat. If it is still tough, secure the lid again. Press Cancel, then Manual, and add an additional 5 minutes of cook time. When the Instant Pot beeps, carefully switch the steam release valve to Venting to quick-release the pressure. When fully released, open the lid. Use tongs to remove the brisket to a dish and loosely cover.

7. Press Cancel. Taste the liquid in the Instant Pot. Add salt to taste. (If it is too salty already, dilute it with water or broth.) Place the cabbage in the cooking liquid. Secure the lid and turn the steam release valve to Sealing. Press the Pressure Cook or Manual button and set the cook time to 3 minutes (or up to 5 minutes if you prefer softer cabbage).

8. When the Instant Pot beeps, carefully switch the steam release valve to Venting to quick-release the pressure. When fully released, open the lid. Use tongs to remove the cabbage to a serving platter.

9. Slice the brisket across the grain into slices ½ inch thick. Arrange it on the serving platter with the cabbage. Strain the cooking liquid and put it in a gravy boat. Serve with the gravy and horseradish sauce on the side.

FOR SERVING

1 small head cabbage (green or red), cut into 8 wedges through the core

MACRONUTRIENTS PER SERVING

FOR BRISKET AND CABBAGE

CALORIES: 378

FAT: 16 G/144 CALORIES

CARBOHYDRATE: 2 G/8 CALORIES

PROTEIN: 54 G/216 CALORIES

FOR HORSERADISH SAUCE

CALORIES: 43

FAT: 4 G/36 CALORIES

CARBOHYDRATE: 1 G/4 CALORIES

PROTEIN: 1 G/4 CALORIES

LOWCOUNTRY BOIL
[PAGE 136]

Lowcountry boils are an institution throughout the Gulf Coast of the United States. During the summer months, friends and family gather around abundant piles of hot seafood and vegetables spread across newspaper-covered tables (often featuring a hole in the middle, beneath which sits a trash receptacle for collecting seafood shells). Traditional Lowcountry boils typically include corn and potatoes, but this recipe omits the corn and uses radish to replace the potato. Feel free to experiment with any other nonstarchy root vegetable in place of the radish if you like.

LOWCOUNTRY BOIL

MAKES 6 SERVINGS

1 medium onion, halved

4 cloves garlic, smashed

8 ounces radishes, trimmed and halved

1 (12- to 14-ounce) package smoked or andouille sausage, cut into 1-inch pieces

8 ounces white mushrooms

1 pound crawfish (or more shrimp)

1 (3-ounce) package Cajun-style crab boil seasoning

4 cups chicken bone broth (see page 32), stock, or filtered water

1 pound large shrimp, fresh or frozen

1. Place the onion and garlic in the Instant Pot. Add the radish, sausage, mushrooms, and crawfish to the pot. In a bowl, stir the crab boil seasoning into the broth to dissolve. Pour the broth mixture over the ingredients in the pot.

2. Secure the lid and set the steam release valve to Sealing. Press the Pressure Cook or Manual button and set the cook time to 3 minutes.

3. When the Instant Pot beeps, carefully switch the steam release valve to Venting to quick-release the pressure. When fully released, open the lid and add the shrimp. Secure the lid and allow the shrimp to cook on Keep Warm for 3 minutes for fresh or 5 minutes for frozen. Check to see if the shrimp are opaque. If not, replace the lid and cook for about 2 minutes more. (If the liquid in the pot cools down too much, switch to the Sauté function to warm it back up.)

4. Discard the onion and garlic and serve immediately, family-style. For the full experience, enjoy this meal outside and eat with your hands.

MACRONUTRIENTS PER SERVING

CALORIES: 321

FAT: 12 G/109 CALORIES

CARBOHYDRATE: 6 G/23 CALORIES

PROTEIN: 46 G/182 CALORIES

This fragrant Indian-style curry is sure to please even the pickiest eaters. If you don't have lamb, any protein (or even vegetables) can be used as a substitute, just adjust the cooking times accordingly. Serve this over Cauliflower Rice (page 36).

LAMB KORMA

MAKES 6 SERVINGS

- 2 tablespoons ghee or coconut oil
- ½ medium onion, chopped
- 1 (6-inch) Anaheim chile, minced
- 1 clove garlic, grated
- ½ teaspoon grated fresh ginger
- 2 teaspoons ground cumin
- 1 teaspoon coriander seeds
- 1 teaspoon garam masala
- 1 teaspoon sea salt
- ½ teaspoon cayenne pepper
- ¼ teaspoon ground cardamom (see Note)

  Pinch of ground cinnamon
- ½ tablespoon tomato paste
- 1 cup chicken bone broth (see page 32) or stock
- 3 pounds lamb shoulder, cut into 1-inch cubes
- ¼ cup full-fat coconut milk
- ½ cup Homemade Dairy Yogurt (page 180), Homemade Coconut Yogurt (page 182), or full-fat Greek yogurt

1. Set the Instant Pot to Sauté. When hot, add the ghee, onion, chile, garlic, and ginger and sauté for 2 minutes, stirring frequently. Add the cumin, coriander seeds, garam masala, salt, cayenne, cardamom, cinnamon, and tomato paste and sauté until sweetly fragrant, 1 minute longer. Deglaze the pot with the broth, scraping the bottom with a wooden spoon to loosen any browned bits. Add the lamb and stir well. Press Cancel.

2. Secure the lid and turn the steam release valve to Sealing. Press the Pressure Cook or Manual button and set the cook time to 15 minutes.

3. When the Instant Pot beeps, carefully switch the steam release valve to Venting to quick-release the pressure. When fully released, open the lid. Stir in the coconut milk and yogurt. Press Cancel and then Sauté and allow the mixture to simmer gently for 5 minutes longer, stirring occasionally until the desired consistency is reached. Serve hot.

NOTE: Instead of using preground cardamom, you can split the seeds out of 2 cardamom pods and grind with a mortar and pestle.

MACRONUTRIENTS PER SERVING

| CALORIES: 709 |
| FAT: 52 G/471 CALORIES |
| CARBOHYDRATE: 4 G/16 CALORIES |
| PROTEIN: 53 G/212 CALORIES |

COQ AU RIESLING

MAKES 6 SERVINGS

4 ounces thick-cut bacon, diced

1 leek, white part only, rinsed and sliced

1 to 2 tablespoons avocado oil (if needed)

1 whole pasture-raised chicken (3 to 4 pounds), cut into 10 pieces

2 teaspoons kosher salt

2 cloves garlic, minced

8 ounces cremini mushrooms, sliced

1 tablespoon chopped fresh tarragon

2 tablespoons chopped fresh parsley

1½ cups dry Riesling

¼ cup Cultured Cream (page 184), crème fraîche, or full-fat coconut milk

MACRONUTRIENTS PER SERVING

CALORIES: 572

FAT: 19 G/171 CALORIES

CARBOHYDRATE: 7 G/28 CALORIES

PROTEIN: 78 G/312 CALORIES

1. Set the Instant Pot to Sauté. Add the bacon and cook until crispy, about 5 minutes. Add the leek and cook until softened, about 10 minutes. While the leek is cooking, pat the chicken dry and season it with the salt. Use a slotted spoon to transfer the bacon and leek to a bowl and set aside, leaving the fat.

2. If the pot looks dry, add the avocado oil. Working in batches, brown the chicken for 3 minutes per side until golden. Transfer the chicken pieces to a platter.

3. Add the garlic, mushrooms, and half of the tarragon and parsley to the pot. Stir to coat the mushrooms in the fat and cook for 1 minute. Deglaze the pot with the wine, scraping the bottom with a wooden spoon to loosen any browned bits. Allow the wine to heat to boiling and cook for 5 minutes. Press Cancel.

4. Return the chicken to the pot along with any accumulated juices. Add the leek-bacon mixture. Secure the lid and set the steam release valve to Sealing. Press the Pressure Cook or Manual button and set the cook time to 8 minutes.

5. When the Instant Pot beeps, carefully switch the steam release valve to Venting to quick-release the pressure. When fully released, open the lid. Transfer the chicken pieces and vegetables to a platter or serving plates.

6. Press Cancel, then Sauté. Stir the cultured cream into the liquid in the pot. Allow the sauce to thicken 2 to 3 minutes, then carefully pour it into a gravy boat or small serving bowl. Garnish the chicken and vegetables with the remaining fresh herbs. Serve with the braising sauce on the side.

So tender you can pull it apart, with vegetables so perfectly cooked you'll be excited for leftovers. If you are strictly limiting carbs, you can omit the sweet potato, or better yet, leave it in for cooking but opt not to eat any.

PERFECT POT ROAST

MAKES 6 SERVINGS

3-pound grass-fed beef chuck roast

2 teaspoons sea salt or Himalayan pink salt

6 tablespoons avocado oil or melted beef tallow

½ teaspoon celery salt

½ teaspoon smoked paprika

½ teaspoon onion powder

½ teaspoon dried parsley flakes

¼ teaspoon ground white pepper

2 cups beef bone broth (see page 32) or vegetable broth

1 small red onion, thinly sliced

2 stalks celery, including leaves, cut into 1-inch pieces

1 medium sweet potato, peeled and cut into ½-inch cubes

1. Sprinkle the roast with salt and ideally allow it to sit at room temperature for 30 to 60 minutes.

2. Set the Instant Pot to Sauté and add ¼ cup of the oil, swirling to coat the bottom of the pot. When the oil is hot, place the roast inside and sear it for 3 minutes, then flip it and sear for 3 minutes on the second side.

3. While the roast sears, in a small bowl, mix the celery salt, smoked paprika, onion powder, parsley, and white pepper.

4. Use heavy-duty tongs to carefully remove the roast to a large bowl. Deglaze the pot with about ¼ cup broth, scraping the bottom with a wooden spoon to loosen any browned bits.

5. Pour in the remaining broth and add all but 1 teaspoon of the spice mixture. Stir in the onion and celery. Return the roast to the pot.

6. Press cancel. Secure the lid and set the steam release valve to Sealing. Press the Meat/Stew button, making sure the pressure is set to High. (If it is not, press the Meat/Stew button 1 or 2 more times until High pressure is selected.) Adjust the cook time to 70 minutes.

7. While the roast cooks, in a medium bowl, combine the sweet potato, turnip, and squash and drizzle with the remaining 2 tablespoons oil. Season with the reserved 1 teaspoon of the spice mix. Stir well to coat the vegetables with the oil and spices. Allow to sit at room temperature.

8. When the Instant Pot beeps, allow the pressure to release naturally for 10 minutes, then carefully switch the steam release valve to Venting. When fully released, open the lid. Carefully remove the roast to a cutting board to rest.

9. Press Cancel. Add the sweet potato, turnip, and squash to the liquid in the pot. Secure the lid and set the steam release valve to Sealing. Press the Pressure Cook or Manual button and set the cook time to 3 minutes.

10. When the Instant Pot beeps, carefully switch the steam release valve to Venting to quick-release the pressure. When fully released, open the lid and stir the contents.

11. Slice the roast across the grain, or pull it apart with tongs. Divide the meat among six serving bowls. Ladle a generous portion of the broth and vegetables from the pot on top of the meat. Garnish with fresh parsley and serve hot.

1 medium turnip, peeled and cut into ½-inch cubes

2 small yellow squash, cut into ½-inch slices

3 tablespoons finely chopped fresh parsley leaves (optional)

MACRONUTRIENTS PER SERVING

CALORIES: 720

FAT: 56 G/504 CALORIES

CARBOHYDRATE: 7 G/30 CALORIES

PROTEIN: 45 G/180 CALORIES

These dumplings have a Cantonese-style filing that includes shrimp, pork, and mushrooms. Kids and adults love these equally. Consider doubling the recipe, and recruit the kids to help you roll the shumai!

CABBAGE SHUMAI

8   large outer cabbage leaves (Savoy recommended)

FOR THE FILLING

10   ounces ground pork

½   pound shrimp, peeled, deveined, and finely chopped

2   dried shiitake mushrooms, soaked to rehydrate, minced

1   large egg

1   tablespoon coconut vinegar

1   tablespoon tamari or coconut aminos

1   teaspoon sesame oil

1   scallion, white and light-green parts only, minced

1   teaspoon grated fresh ginger

Pinch of ground black pepper

1   cup water

MACRONUTRIENTS PER SHUMAI

CALORIES: 86

FAT: 5 G/44 CALORIES

CARBOHYDRATE: 2 G/7 CALORIES

PROTEIN: 9 G/35 CALORIES

1. Bring a large pot of water to a boil on the stove. Set up a large bowl of ice water. Blanch the cabbage by boiling the leaves for 1 minute, then dunking them in a bowl of ice water to stop the cooking process. This should make the leaves pliable.

2. Halve each leaf lengthwise and remove the tough center rib. Blot any excess moisture from the leaves with a clean kitchen towel and set these "shumai wrappers" aside.

3. For the filling: In a bowl, combine the pork, shrimp, mushrooms, egg, vinegar, tamari, sesame oil, scallion, ginger, and pepper and stir in one direction until the mixture comes together in a ball. Toss the mixture between your hands a few times to help the filling set.

4. Place about 1 tablespoon of filling in the center of one piece of cabbage wrapper. Roll the cabbage burrito-style: Begin by tightly folding in the left and right sides. Next, fold the bottom edge up over the filling snugly. Finally, roll the wrap away from you. Set the completed wrap on a plate seam side down so that it does not unroll. Continue until all the filling is used.

5. Pour the water into the Instant Pot. Place the metal steam rack/trivet inside. Place a steaming basket atop the trivet. Arrange the cabbage rolls inside the basket, seam side down. Secure the lid and set the steam release valve to Sealing. Press the Pressure Cook or Manual button and set the cook time to 9 minutes.

6. Meanwhile, for the dipping sauce: In a bowl, whisk together the tamari, vinegar, sesame oil, and pepper flakes.

7. When the Instant Pot beeps, carefully switch the steam release valve to Venting to quick-release the pressure. When fully released, open the lid. Use tongs to transfer the cabbage shumai to a serving plate.

8. Serve the cabbage shumai warm, with individual bowls of sauce for dunking.

FOR THE DIPPING SAUCE

- ¼ cup tamari or coconut aminos
- 2 tablespoons coconut vinegar
- 2 teaspoons sesame oil
- ½ teaspoon red pepper flakes

Marinated in mustard and turmeric, cooked with lemon and garlic, and topped off with olives and capers? Sounds like a Mediterranean vacation for my mouth.

CHICKEN THIGHS WITH OLIVES AND CAPERS

MAKES 6 SERVINGS

6   bone-in, skinless chicken thighs (about 3 pounds; see Note)

1   teaspoon kosher salt

3   tablespoons avocado oil

¾   teaspoon ground turmeric

½   teaspoon ground black pepper

¼   teaspoon sweet paprika

¼   teaspoon mustard powder

1   large or 2 small lemons

2   tablespoons ghee or fat of choice

1   cup chicken bone broth (see page 32)

2   cloves garlic, chopped

¾   cup pitted olives (green, black, kalamata, or a mix)

2   tablespoons capers

3   tablespoons finely chopped fresh parsley leaves (optional)

MACRONUTRIENTS PER SERVING

CALORIES: 331

FAT: 24 G/216 CALORIES

CARBOHYDRATE: 4 G/16 CALORIES

PROTEIN: 25 G/100 CALORIES

1. Season the top and bottom of the chicken thighs with the salt. Place them in a shallow baking dish.

2. In a small bowl, mix together the avocado oil, turmeric, black pepper, paprika, and mustard powder. Spoon about half of this mixture over the bottom side of the chicken. Flip the thighs. Spoon the rest of the marinade over the top. Allow the chicken to marinate for 20 to 30 minutes at room temperature or up to 8 hours in the refrigerator.

3. Thinly slice half the lemon and set the other half aside.

4. Set the Instant Pot to Sauté and heat the ghee, swirling to coat the bottom of the pot. Place 3 thighs skin side down in the pot. Brown for 3 minutes undisturbed, then flip and brown 2 minutes on the second side. Remove to a plate. Repeat with the rest of the chicken. Transfer the second batch to the plate.

5. Carefully pour in about ¼ cup of the bone broth to deglaze the pot, scraping the bottom with a wooden spoon to loosen any browned bits. Press Cancel.

6. Arrange the lemon slices on the bottom of pot and layer the chicken over the top, overlapping them to fit if needed. Do not try to force them into a single layer. Pour any reserved juices from the plate and any reserved marinade over the chicken, along with the remaining ¾ cup bone broth. Squeeze the other half of the lemon over the top and place the spent rind in the pot. Toss the garlic, olives, and capers around the chicken.

7. Secure the lid and turn the steam release valve to Sealing. Press the Pressure Cook or Manual button and set the cook time to 14 minutes.

8. When the Instant Pot beeps, carefully switch the steam release valve to Venting to quick-release the pressure. When fully released, open the lid. Use tongs to transfer the chicken to a shallow baking dish for serving. Taste the cooking liquid and adjust the seasoning. Carefully ladle the cooking liquid with the olives and capers over top of the chicken, and garnish with parsley if desired. Enjoy!

NOTE: If you want to use skin-on chicken, follow the same directions as above, spooning some of the marinade under the skin in step 2. The reason the recipe calls for skinless is that chicken skin simply doesn't stay crispy in the Instant Pot. For crispy skin, you will want to stick your chicken under a hot broiler for a minute after it has been cooked.

Cuts of meat like short ribs require a long cooking time in the oven to become tender. Cooking them under pressure reduces the cook time dramatically with the same end results—tender meat that practically melts in your mouth.

SHORT RIBS WITH RADISHES

1 teaspoon kosher salt

½ teaspoon smoked paprika

¼ teaspoon ground coriander

¼ teaspoon ground cumin

Pinch of ground allspice (optional)

4 bone-in beef short ribs (2 to 2½ pounds total)

2 tablespoons bacon fat, or fat or oil of choice

1 cup filtered water

2 bunches radishes, ends trimmed, leaves thoroughly washed and roughly chopped (see Note)

Freshly ground black pepper

MACRONUTRIENTS PER SERVING

CALORIES: 404

FAT: 29 G/261 CALORIES

CARBOHYDRATE: 4 G/16 CALORIES

PROTEIN: 30 G/120 CALORIES

NOTE: Choose smaller radishes if you can. If your radishes are large, cut them in half before cooking.

1. In a small bowl, mix together the salt, paprika, coriander, cumin, and allspice. Rub the spice blend over the surface of the short ribs.

2. Set the Instant Pot to Sauté and add the fat. When it starts to smoke, add the short ribs bone side up. Brown for 4 to 5 minutes. Flip, and brown 4 minutes on the second side. Press Cancel.

3. Pour the water into the Instant Pot. Secure the lid and turn the steam release valve to Sealing. Press the Pressure Cook or Manual button and set the cook time to 45 minutes.

4. When the Instant Pot beeps, allow the pressure to release naturally for 10 minutes, then carefully switch the steam release valve to Venting. When fully released, open the lid. Remove the short ribs to a serving plate and cover loosely.

5. Press Cancel. Add the radishes to the liquid in the pot. Place a metal steaming basket directly on top of the radishes and place the greens in the basket.

6. Secure the lid and set the steam release valve to Sealing. Press the Pressure Cook or Manual button and set the cook time to 3 minutes (or up to 5 minutes if you prefer softer radishes).

7. When the Instant Pot beeps, carefully switch the steam release valve to Venting to quick-release the pressure. When fully released, open the lid. Use tongs to transfer the greens to a serving bowl. Taste and season with salt and pepper. Use a slotted spoon to remove the radishes and place them on top of the greens. Serve hot with the short ribs.

We've adapted Naked Chicken Kiev from a recipe on my blog, *Mark's Daily Apple* (marksdailyapple.com). This buttery, herby preparation will make you excited about chicken breasts again!

NAKED CHICKEN KIEV

MAKES 4 SERVINGS

10 tablespoons unsalted butter, at room temperature

1 tablespoon minced fresh parsley

1 teaspoon dried dillweed

Sea salt and ground black pepper

4 boneless, skinless chicken breasts (about 6 ounces each)

1 cup water

MACRONUTRIENTS PER SERVING

CALORIES: 490

FAT: 35 G/315 CALORIES

CARBOHYDRATE: 1 G/4 CALORIES

PROTEIN: 42 G/168 CALORIES

1. In a bowl, mix together 8 tablespoons of the butter, the parsley, dill, and ¼ teaspoon each salt and pepper until well combined. Scoop the butter onto a sheet of parchment paper or plastic wrap and roll into a log about the size of a stick of butter. Freeze for 25 minutes to firm up.

2. Meanwhile, if the chicken breasts are very thick, butterfly them open with a sharp knife. Place each chicken breast between two sheets of parchment paper or plastic wrap and pound to a ¼-inch thickness using a mallet or rolling pin. Be careful not to pound the chicken too thin or it will tear.

3. Remove the butter from the freezer and slice it into 4 equal-size rectangular pieces. Place a piece of butter in the middle of each chicken breast. Fold in the sides to slightly cover the butter, then roll up from bottom to top to form a tight roll, like a burrito. Secure with a toothpick (optional). Place the chicken breasts in a glass dish seam side down and refrigerate for 1 hour. This helps keep the rolls from falling apart during cooking. (See Note.)

4. Remove the chicken from the refrigerator and season the outside of the rolls with a generous pinch each of salt and pepper.

5. Set the Instant Pot to Sauté and heat the remaining 2 tablespoons butter. When the butter has stopped foaming, press Cancel, re-select Sauté, and adjust the heat to Less. Add

the chicken breasts seam side down. Cook for 2 to 3 minutes per side until nicely browned on the top and bottom. Press Cancel.

6. Place the chicken breasts in a stainless steel, Pyrex, or silicone baking dish that fits inside your Instant Pot. Pour the butter from the pot over the chicken. If your metal steam rack/trivet does not have handles, make a sling (see Note, page 42).

7. Pour the water into the pot. Place the steam rack/trivet inside and arrange the sling over it so the two ends stick up like handles, then lower the baking dish onto the sling and rack. Secure the lid and set the steam release valve to Sealing. Press the Pressure Cook or Manual button and set the cook time to 6 minutes.

8. When the Instant Pot beeps, allow the pressure to release naturally for 5 minutes, then carefully switch the steam release valve to Venting to quick-release the pressure. When fully released, open the lid. Use tongs to transfer the chicken to serving plates and pour the butter from the baking dish over the chicken. Allow to rest for a few minutes before serving.

NOTE: Steps 1 through 3 can be done in advance. The rolled stuffed breasts can be stored in airtight containers in the refrigerator or wrapped in freezer paper and frozen for quick cooking later.

This recipe is an excellent choice for cooking ahead if you like to prepare meals for the workweek, as it reheats very well. Serve atop a bed of Cauliflower Rice (page 36) or fresh greens for a complete meal.

CHICKEN TINGA

2 tablespoons avocado oil

½ onion, chopped

3 cloves garlic, smashed

3 Roma (plum) tomatoes, chopped

½ cup chicken bone broth (see page 32)

3 chipotle peppers in adobo sauce plus ½ tablespoon adobo sauce (see Note)

1 tablespoon fresh lime juice

½ teaspoon ground cumin

½ teaspoon dried oregano

Sea salt and ground black pepper

2 pounds boneless, skinless chicken (breast, thigh, or both), cut into 1-inch pieces

2 bay leaves

MACRONUTRIENTS PER SERVING

CALORIES: 293

FAT: 10 G/90 CALORIES

CARBOHYDRATE: 4 G/16 CALORIES

PROTEIN: 47 G/188 CALORIES

1. Set the Instant Pot to Sauté and heat the oil. Add the onion and cook 3 minutes, stirring frequently. Add the garlic and cook until fragrant, 1 minute longer. Add the tomatoes and cook until they begin to break down slightly, 2 to 3 minutes. Deglaze the pot with the broth, scraping the bottom with a wooden spoon to loosen any browned bits. Press Cancel.

2. Pour the broth mixture into a blender or food processor and add the chipotle peppers, adobo sauce, lime juice, cumin, and oregano. Process until smooth. Taste the sauce and season with salt and black pepper to taste.

3. Lay the chicken in the Instant Pot, add the bay leaves, and pour the blended sauce on top. Toss to coat the chicken. Secure the lid and set the steam release valve to Sealing. Press the Pressure Cook or Manual button and set the cook time to 10 minutes.

4. When the Instant Pot beeps, carefully switch the steam release valve to Venting to quick-release the pressure. When fully released, open the lid. Discard the bay leaves. Shred the chicken with two forks, mixing it with the sauce. Serve warm.

NOTE: The spice level of this dish can be adjusted by adding or removing chipotle peppers and adobo sauce to suit your tastes.

If you are cooking shrimp in the Instant Pot, start with frozen shrimp to avoid overcooking the delicate meat.

CREAMY SHRIMP PRIMAVERA

MAKES 2 SERVINGS

2 tablespoons unsalted butter or avocado oil

¼ medium onion, diced

4 cloves garlic, minced

1 cup chicken bone broth (see page 32) or stock

2 cups broccoli florets

4 ounces cherry tomatoes, halved

4 ounces white mushrooms, sliced

1 small zucchini, sliced on a diagonal

10 ounces frozen large shrimp, peeled and deveined

½ cup heavy whipping cream or full-fat coconut milk

½ teaspoon lemon zest

1 teaspoon sea salt

½ teaspoon ground black pepper

½ cup grated Parmesan cheese or nutritional yeast

¼ cup fresh basil chiffonade (see Note, page 92)

MACRONUTRIENTS PER SERVING

CALORIES: 658

FAT: 42 G/378 CALORIES

CARBOHYDRATE: 24 G/96 CALORIES

PROTEIN: 50 G/200 CALORIES

1. Set the Instant Pot to Sauté and heat the butter until foaming. Add the onion and sauté until just golden, about 2 minutes. Add the garlic and sauté 1 minute more. Deglaze the pot with the broth, scraping the bottom with a wooden spoon to loosen any browned bits. Press Cancel.

2. Layer the broccoli, tomatoes, mushrooms, and zucchini in a deep stainless steel or Pyrex cooking dish that fits in your Instant Pot. Place the shrimp atop the vegetables. If your metal steam rack/trivet does not have handles, make a sling (see Note, page 42). Carefully set the steam rack/trivet into the liquid and arrange the sling over it so the two ends stick up like handles, then lower the dish onto the sling and rack.

3. Secure the lid and set the steam release valve to Sealing. Press the Pressure Cook or Manual button and set the cook time to 2 minutes.

4. When the Instant Pot beeps, carefully switch the steam release valve to Venting to quick-release the pressure. When fully released, open the lid. Use the sling to carefully remove the dish, and gloves or tongs to remove the rack. Set aside.

5. Press the Sauté button and pour in the cream, lemon zest, salt, and pepper. Cook for 1 minute, stirring frequently, or longer if you prefer a thicker sauce. Taste and adjust the salt and pepper.

6. Transfer the shrimp and vegetables to a large serving bowl, discarding any liquid. Ladle the cream sauce over top and toss together. Add the Parmesan and toss once more. Garnish with the fresh basil and serve immediately.

Tri-tip is one of my favorite cuts of beef. I generally cook it on an outdoor grill, but I also love the tender, juicy results you get from cooking it in the Instant Pot. It's a whole different spin on tri-tip! Serve the tri-tip with Garlic Mashed Rutabaga (page 100) and Brussels Sprouts with Pancetta and Nuts (page 109) for an absolutely killer meal.

BRAISED TRI-TIP

MAKES 4 SERVINGS

2 pound tri-tip steak

2 teaspoons coarse sea salt

3 tablespoons avocado oil, plus more if needed

½ medium onion, diced

2 cloves garlic, smashed

1 tablespoon tomato paste

1½ cups dry red wine such as Cabernet Sauvignon or Merlot or beef bone broth (see page 32)

½ tablespoon dried thyme

2 bay leaves

1 Roma (plum) tomato, diced

1 stalk celery including leaves, chopped

1 small carrot, chopped

½ cup filtered water or bone broth (see page 32)

MACRONUTRIENTS PER SERVING

CALORIES: 599

FAT: 31 G/275 CALORIES

CARBOHYDRATE: 8 G/33 CALORIES

PROTEIN: 49 G/196 CALORIES

1. Pat the tri-tip dry with paper towels and season with the coarse salt. Set the Instant Pot to Sauté and heat the avocado oil until shimmering. Cook the steak for about 2 minutes per side, until deeply golden. Remove the steak from the pot and place it in a shallow bowl. Set aside.

2. Add more oil if the pot is dry, then add the onion to the pot and cook for 3 minutes, stirring frequently. Add the garlic and sauté for 1 minute. Add the tomato paste and cook 1 minute longer, stirring constantly.

3. Deglaze the pot with the red wine, scraping the bottom with a wooden spoon to loosen any browned bits. Stir in the thyme and bay leaves. Press Cancel.

4. Return the tri-tip steak to the pot along with any accumulated juices from bowl. Scatter the tomato, celery, and carrot around the steak. Pour in the water. Secure the lid and set the steam release valve to Sealing. Press the Pressure Cook or Manual button and set the cook time to 35 minutes.

5. When the Instant Pot beeps, allow the pressure to release naturally for 20 minutes, then carefully switch the steam release valve to Venting. When fully released, open the lid. Discard the bay leaves.

6. Remove the steak and place it in a covered dish to rest. While the steak is resting, press the Sauté button and allow

the braising liquid to come to a boil. Cook until the liquid is reduced by about half, about 10 minutes. Press Cancel.

7. If desired, use an immersion blender to carefully the blend the hot braising liquid for a smoother sauce.

8. Slice the steak thinly across the grain and serve with a generous ladle of braising liquid over top.

Sausage and peppers are delicious enough on their own, but add Roma tomatoes and Parmesan cheese and you have a house favorite, perfect for gatherings or for when cooler autumn and winter nights come calling.

SAUSAGE AND PEPPERS

2 tablespoons extra-virgin olive oil or avocado oil

1 pound mild or hot Italian sausage links

2 cups Red Sauce (page 93) or 2½ cups store-bought keto-friendly marinara

½ cup bone broth (see page 32; omit if using store-bought marinara)

1 Roma (plum) tomato, diced

2 green bell peppers, cut into thick strips

¾ cup grated or shredded Parmesan cheese

Pinch of red pepper flakes

MACRONUTRIENTS PER SERVING

WITH RED SAUCE
CALORIES: 629
FAT: 48 G/428 CALORIES
CARBOHYDRATE: 16 G/64 CALORIES
PROTEIN: 32 G/128 CALORIES

1. Set the Instant Pot to Sauté and add the oil. When it starts to smoke, add the sausages. Sauté until browned, 2 to 3 minutes per side. Press Cancel.

2. Carefully pour in the red sauce and bone broth (if using) and stir to mix. Layer the diced tomato and bell peppers on top of the sausages without mixing.

3. Secure the lid and set the steam release valve to Sealing. Press the Pressure Cook or Manual button and set the cook time to 10 minutes.

4. When the Instant Pot beeps, allow the pressure to release naturally for 5 minutes, then carefully switch the steam release valve to Venting to quick-release the pressure. When fully released, open the lid. Use tongs to remove the sausages and peppers and arrange them on a serving platter. Stir the sauce in the Instant Pot. If you would like it thicker, press Cancel, then Sauté, and simmer the sauce until it reaches the desired consistency. Ladle the sauce over the sausages. Sprinkle the Parmesan and pepper flakes over the top and serve hot.

The first time I tried it, I thought salmon would come out dry in the Instant Pot. Boy, was I wrong! You can even prepare this recipe using still-frozen salmon fillets if you come home after a busy day and realize you have nothing thawed for dinner. Simply increase the cooking time in step 4 to 6 minutes. Yes, really!

SALMON WITH HERBY YOGURT SAUCE

MAKES 4 SERVINGS

FOR THE YOGURT SAUCE

- 1 English cucumber, striped (lightly peeled), seeded, and shredded
- ¼ teaspoon kosher salt
- 1 small lemon
- 1 tablespoon finely chopped fresh parsley leaves (stems reserved; see Note)
- 1 tablespoon finely chopped fresh mint leaves (stems reserved; see Note)
- 1 tablespoon finely chopped fresh dill (stems reserved; see Note) or 1 teaspoon dried dillweed
- ¾ cup Homemade Dairy Yogurt (page 180), Homemade Coconut Yogurt (page 182), or full-fat Greek yogurt
- 1 teaspoon extra-virgin olive oil

  Freshly ground black pepper

1. For the yogurt sauce: Place the shredded cucumber in a sieve set over a bowl. Sprinkle with the kosher salt and toss gently. Set aside. Zest and juice the lemon. Measure out 2 teaspoons of juice. Reserve the spent lemon rind and any extra juice for step 3.

2. Use a spatula to press the excess liquid out of the cucumber. Transfer the cucumber to a bowl and add the lemon zest, 2 teaspoons lemon juice, parsley, mint, dill, yogurt, olive oil, and salt and pepper to taste. Stir well and refrigerate until serving time (see Note).

3. For the salmon: Pour the water into the Instant Pot. Add the fresh herb stems (along with a few extra sprigs of herbs if you have them) and spent lemon rind. Place the metal steam rack/trivet inside. Arrange the salmon skin side down on the rack. Pour any leftover lemon juice and the melted butter over the salmon. Season generously with sea salt and pepper. Place 2 slices of lemon on each piece of salmon.

4. Secure the lid and turn the steam release valve to Sealing. Select the Steam function and set the cook time to 3 minutes.

5. When the Instant Pot beeps, carefully switch the steam release valve to Venting to quick-release the pressure. When fully released, open the lid. Gently lift out the trivet with the handles, or carefully grab it with tongs if your trivet does not have handles, and transfer the salmon to a serving plate. Remove the lemon slices (reserve for garnish, if desired) and drizzle the salmon with the olive oil.

6. The salmon can be enjoyed warm, or you can allow it to cool for a few minutes, then transfer it to the refrigerator to serve chilled later. Before serving, stir the yogurt sauce. If desired, garnish the salmon with the reserved lemon slices.

NOTES

- When stripping the herb leaves from their stems for the yogurt sauce, save the stems to add to the Instant Pot in step 3.
- For a thicker yogurt sauce, prepare it a few hours ahead of time. Line a fine-mesh sieve with a few layers of cheesecloth or a thin kitchen towel and set it over a bowl. Place the yogurt sauce on the cheesecloth and let it sit in the fridge until serving time.

FOR THE SALMON

- 1 cup water
- 4 skin-on salmon fillets (3 to 4 ounces each)
- 1 tablespoon melted butter or ghee (or more olive oil)

   Sea salt and ground black pepper

- 1 lemon, cut into 8 slices
- 1 tablespoon good-quality extra-virgin olive oil

MACRONUTRIENTS PER SERVING

CALORIES: 212
FAT: 11 G/99 CALORIES
CARBOHYDRATE: 5 G/20 CALORIES
PROTEIN: 24 G/98 CALORIES

This meal is cooked en papillote, or in a paper packet. Open them at the table so that guests can enjoy the delicate aromas of the fish and herbs. For a complete one-pot meal, steam fresh vegetables in the bottom of the pot and cook the fish on a steam rack on top.

MEDITERRANEAN FISH EN PAPILLOTE

MAKES 2 SERVINGS

2 tablespoons avocado oil

2 cloves garlic, thinly sliced

½ cup halved cherry tomatoes

12 marinated mixed olives, halved

1 tablespoon capers, drained

¼ teaspoon dried oregano

2 cod or other delicate white fish fillets (4 to 6 ounces each, thick fillets if possible)

½ teaspoon sea salt

Scant ¼ teaspoon ground black pepper

2 teaspoons melted unsalted butter or extra-virgin olive oil

2 sprigs fresh thyme

½ lemon, cut into 4 thin slices

1 cup water

MACRONUTRIENTS PER SERVING

CALORIES: 386

FAT: 22 G/198 CALORIES

CARBOHYDRATE: 5 G/20 CALORIES

PROTEIN: 42 G/168 CALORIES

1. Cut two 16-inch squares of parchment paper. Fold each piece in half with the cut ends together. Cut each into a heart or semicircle with the crease in the middle.

2. In a skillet, heat the avocado oil over medium heat until warm. Add the garlic and cook, stirring frequently, until golden, about 1 minute. Add the tomatoes and cook 1 minute longer. Remove from the heat and stir in the olives, capers, and oregano.

3. Unfold the parchment paper hearts. Place one fish fillet on each sheet of parchment paper to one side of the fold. Season both sides of the fillets with the salt and pepper. Top each fillet with half of the tomato and olive mixture and the melted butter, 1 thyme sprig, and 2 lemon slices.

4. Seal the parchment paper pouches by folding the empty side over the fish. Starting at the round end of the heart, make a series of small overlapping folds until you reach the heart's tail. When you reach the end, fold this portion underneath.

5. Pour the water into the Instant Pot. Place the metal steam rack/trivet inside. Put the parchment paper pouches on top of the rack. Secure the lid and set the steam release valve to Sealing. Press the Pressure Cook or Manual button and set the cook time to 4 minutes.

6. When the Instant Pot beeps, carefully switch the steam release valve to Venting to quick-release the pressure. When fully released, open the lid. Carefully lift out the packets and place them on a serving platter. Serve the packets immediately.

DESSERTS

164

167

169

It is hard to believe something that tastes this good can also be keto approved!

INDIVIDUAL CRUSTLESS KETO CHEESECAKES

MAKES 4 SERVINGS

2½ tablespoons coconut oil, melted

16 ounces full-fat cream cheese, at room temperature

4 teaspoons vanilla extract

10 to 20 drops of liquid stevia, or to taste (or keto-friendly sweetener of choice)

2 large eggs, at room temperature

1 cup water

3½ ounces dark chocolate (at least 85% cacao), broken into pieces

1 cup Basic Whipped Cream (recipe follows; optional)

1. Use about ½ tablespoon of the coconut oil to grease the bottom and sides of four 6-ounce Pyrex bowls, ceramic rame-kins, or silicone baking cups.

2. In a bowl, with an electric mixer, beat together the cream cheese, vanilla, and 10 drops of stevia. Taste the cheese mixture and add more stevia if desired. Add the eggs and beat for 20 to 30 seconds, until thoroughly combined, but do not overmix.

3. Divide the mixture evenly among the containers. Tap them gently on the countertop to settle the mixture. Cover them with foil or silicone lids.

4. Pour the water into the Instant Pot. Place the metal steam rack/trivet inside. Place the cheesecakes on the rack.

5. Secure the lid and turn the steam release valve to Sealing. Press the Pressure Cook or Manual button and set the cook time to 25 minutes.

6. When the Instant Pot beeps, allow the pressure to release naturally for 10 minutes, then carefully switch the steam release valve to Venting. When fully released, open the lid. Carefully remove the cheesecakes (they will be hot). Place them in the refrigerator for 30 minutes to chill.

7. Place the chocolate and remaining 2 tablespoons coconut oil in a microwave-safe bowl. Microwave on high in 15-second increments, stirring well after each, until the chocolate is melted.

8. Remove the cheesecakes from the refrigerator and spoon the melted chocolate mixture evenly over the cheesecakes. Return them to the refrigerator to chill for an additional 15 to 20 minutes. Serve cold with whipped cream, if desired.

NOTE: To make a single cheesecake instead of individual mini cheesecakes, pour the cheesecake mixture from step 2 into a greased 6- to 7-inch stainless steel, Pyrex, or silicone baking dish that fits inside your Instant Pot. Cover it with foil or a silicone lid and cook as directed.

MACRONUTRIENTS PER SERVING

NO WHIPPED CREAM

CALORIES: 678

FAT: 63 G/568 CALORIES

CARBOHYDRATE: 15 G/60 CALORIES

PROTEIN: 13 G/52 CALORIES

WITH WHIPPED CREAM

CALORIES: 884

FAT: 85 G/761 CALORIES

CARBOHYDRATE: 17 G/67 CALORIES

PROTEIN: 15 G/59 CALORIES

BASIC WHIPPED CREAM

MAKES 2 CUPS

1. Optional but recommended: Place the bowl and the beaters from your electric mixer in the freezer for at least 30 minutes. You can also nest your bowl inside a larger bowl filled partway with ice.

2. Place all the ingredients in the chilled bowl and beat for 1 minute on medium speed until stiff peaks form. Do not overbeat.

1 cup heavy whipping cream

1 teaspoon vanilla extract

2 to 3 drops of liquid stevia, or to taste

If you want a sweet treat but don't want a whole batch of cupcakes sitting around tempting you, this is the perfect solution! Using this cupcake recipe as a starting point, let your imagination run wild concocting your own flavor variations.

STRAWBERRY CUPCAKES

MAKES 2 SERVINGS

FOR THE CAKE

1½   teaspoons coconut oil, melted

2   large eggs

2   tablespoons salted butter, melted

2   tablespoons unsweetened almond milk

½   teaspoon vanilla or almond extract

⅓   cup blanched almond flour

¾   teaspoon baking powder

10   drops of liquid stevia (or keto-friendly sweetener of choice)

2   large strawberries, fresh or frozen and thawed, finely chopped

1   cup water

MACRONUTRIENTS PER SERVING

CALORIES: 527

FAT: 50 G/447 CALORIES

CARBOHYDRATE: 11 G/42 CALORIES

PROTEIN: 13 G/52 CALORIES

1. For the cake: Use the coconut oil to grease the bottom and sides of two silicone muffin cups (preferred), or two small glass jars or bowls.

2. In a small bowl, lightly beat the eggs. Mix in the melted butter, almond milk, vanilla, almond flour, baking powder, and stevia. Set aside a little bit of strawberry for garnish if you want, then fold the chopped strawberries into the batter. Divide the batter evenly between the muffin cups and cover them loosely with foil.

3. Pour the water into the Instant Pot. Place the metal steam rack/trivet inside. If you have a 6-inch metal cake pan, place that on the rack. Place the muffin cups on the rack or pan.

4. Secure the lid and set the steam release valve to Sealing. Press the Pressure Cook or Manual button and set the cook time to 25 minutes.

5. When the Instant Pot beeps, allow the pressure to release naturally for 10 minutes, then carefully switch the steam release valve to Venting. When fully released, open the lid. Carefully remove the cakes (they will be hot). Allow them to cool for about 15 minutes.

6. Meanwhile, for the frosting: In a medium bowl, with an electric mixer, beat together the cream cheese and butter for about 20 seconds. Split the vanilla bean lengthwise and scrape the vanilla seeds into the bowl. Add 2 teaspoons of almond

milk, the monkfruit sweetener, and 5 drops of stevia. Mix for about 20 seconds more until completely combined. Taste and adjust the sweetness as desired, then beat the frosting on high until it is fluffy, 1½ to 2 minutes. If the frosting becomes too thick, beat in the remaining 1 teaspoon of almond milk.

7. When the cakes are cool, spread or pipe the frosting on top of the cakes. Garnish with the reserved strawberry.

NOTE: Choose a brand of monkfruit sweetener that contains only erythritol and monkfruit extract; avoid ones that contain malto-dextrin. You can substitute a powdered keto-friendly sweetener like Swerve brand confectioners sweetener if you are not on a low FODMAP diet.

FOR THE FROSTING

- 2 ounces full-fat cream cheese, at room temperature
- 2 tablespoons unsalted butter, at room temperature
- 2 to 3 teaspoons unsweetened almond milk
- 1 vanilla bean
- 1 teaspoon monkfruit sweetener (see Note)
- 5 to 10 drops of liquid stevia, or to taste

As a keto enthusiast, you are probably already consuming your share of bacon, dark chocolate, nuts, and coconut, but have you ever tried them all together? Sounds crazy, but it works!

BACON DARK CHOCOLATE NUT CLUSTERS

MAKES 12 SERVINGS

½   cup nuts (any type)

2   tablespoons finely shredded coconut, plus 1 tablespoon (optional) for sprinkling

2   slices bacon

2   teaspoons coconut oil

3½   ounces dark chocolate (at least 85% cacao; the darker the better)

¼   teaspoon pink Himalayan sea salt

MACRONUTRIENTS PER SERVING

CALORIES: 101

FAT: 9 G/83 CALORIES

CARBOHYDRATE: 3 G/13 CALORIES

PROTEIN: 2 G/9 CALORIES

1. Set out a 12-cup silicone mini muffin pan (preferred) or line a small baking sheet with parchment paper.

2. In a small food processor, combine the nuts and coconut and pulse a few times to roughly chop. Set aside.

3. Set the Instant Pot to Sauté. When it is hot, add the bacon and cook, flipping occasionally with tongs, until it is crispy. Remove it to a plate.

4. Add the coconut oil to the bacon fat in the pot. Break the chocolate into pieces and place them in the hot oil. Stir with a wooden spoon until the chocolate is melted. Press Cancel and stir in the chopped nuts/coconut mixture. Crumble the bacon into the chocolate mixture and stir to combine.

5. Spoon the chocolate mixture into the mini muffin cups or drop spoonfuls onto the parchment. Sprinkle the pink sea salt and the remaining coconut (if using) over the top.

6. Place the chocolate mixture into the refrigerator to harden for 30 minutes. Remove the clusters from the cups or baking sheet. Store in an airtight container in the refrigerator or freezer. Serve cool so the clusters do not melt.

It's amazing that such simple ingredients can turn into something so delicious and, in this version, keto friendly! I provided a few recipe ideas on the following pages for using this delicious, sunny curd.

LEMON CURD

6 tablespoons unsalted butter

⅔ cup erythritol (or equivalent keto-friendly sweetener of choice)

2 large eggs

2 large egg yolks

⅔ cup fresh lemon juice (see Note)

1 cup water

2 teaspoons grated lemon zest

MACRONUTRIENTS PER 2-TABLESPOON SERVING

CALORIES: 45

FAT: 4 G/36 CALORIES

CARBOHYDRATE: 7 G/28 CALORIES

PROTEIN: 1 G/4 CALORIES

1. In a bowl, with an electric mixer, cream the butter and erythritol until it reaches a completely smooth and uniform consistency, about 3 minutes. With the mixer running, gradually beat in the whole eggs and yolks and mix until just combined. Do not overmix.

2. Mix in the lemon juice until combined. This will cause the mixture to curdle.

3. Place the mixture in a heatproof container with a lid, such as a pint mason jar (or two half-pint jars). Place the lid atop the mouth of the jar without tightening it or cover it with foil; this will keep condensation out of the curd during cooking.

4. Pour the water into the Instant Pot. Place the metal steam rack/trivet inside. Place the jar on the rack. Secure the lid and set the steam release valve to Sealing. Press the Pressure Cook or Manual button and set the cook time to 10 minutes.

5. When the Instant Pot beeps, allow the pressure to release naturally for 10 minutes, then carefully switch the steam release valve to Venting. When fully released, open the lid.

6. Carefully remove the jar (it will be hot!) and stir in the zest until smooth. Allow the curd to cool at room temperature, then cover tightly with the lid and refrigerate. Chill overnight before serving.

NOTE: Be sure to grate the zest needed before squeezing the lemons for juice.

This celebratory recipe makes use of homemade crème fraîche and lemon curd. Trifles can be prepared in advance—in fact, they taste best after being allowed to set overnight—making them a perfect special occasion dessert to serve to guests. You can also use one of the (unfrosted) Strawberry Cupcakes (page 164) instead of the mug cake for a delightful variation.

MINI BERRY LEMON CURD TRIFLES

MAKES 4 SERVINGS

FOR THE MUG CAKE

- 3 tablespoons blanched almond flour
- ½ teaspoon baking powder
- ⅛ teaspoon ground cinnamon
- 1 large egg
- 1 tablespoon salted butter, melted
- 1 tablespoon unsweetened almond milk
- 4 to 5 drops of liquid stevia (or keto-friendly sweetener of choice)
- ¼ teaspoon vanilla extract

  Pinch of sea salt

FOR THE CREAM FILLING

- ¾ cup Cultured Cream (page 184) or crème fraîche
- 1 to 3 drops of liquid stevia (or keto-friendly sweetener of choice), to taste
- 2 drops of vanilla extract

1. For the mug cake: In a small microwave-safe mug or bowl, thoroughly mix the almond flour, baking powder, cinnamon, egg, melted butter, almond milk, stevia, vanilla, and salt. Microwave for 1 minute. Allow the cake to rest for at least 2 minutes, then remove the cake and divide into 4 portions.

2. For the cream filling: In a small bowl, combine the cultured cream, stevia, and vanilla.

3. To assemble the trifles: Set out four 4- to 5-ounce trifle dishes or other small glasses or jars. For each trifle dish:

   a. Cut 1 portion of the mug cake into several thin slices or small cubes. Place half into the bottom of the trifle dish.

(recipe continues)

b. Drizzle the cake with 1 teaspoon lemon curd (dilute the curd with a little bit of warm water if it is too thick to drizzle).

c. Place about 2 tablespoons of the berries over the curd.

d. Top with 1½ tablespoons of the cream filling.

e. Repeat the layering: cake, lemon curd, berries, and cream filling in that order.

4. The trifles can be assemble ahead of time and refrigerated. Before serving, top with a dollop of fresh whipped cream.

TO ASSEMBLE

8 teaspoons Lemon Curd (page 168)

1 cup mixed berries (any kind), fresh or frozen and thawed

4 tablespoons Basic Whipped Cream (page 163)

MACRONUTRIENTS PER SERVING

CALORIES: 316

FAT: 28 G/252 CALORIES

CARBOHYDRATE: 14 G/56 CALORIES

PROTEIN: 5 G/20 CALORIES

This cheesecake is the ultimate pairing of tart and sweet. Try it with both regular and Meyer lemons, which are sweeter. If you don't have the stackable insert pans called for in this recipe, you can bake these cheesecakes in individual ramekins following the directions for Individual Crustless Keto Cheesecakes (page 162) and serve with a dollop of lemon curd on top.

LAYERED LEMON CHEESECAKE

MAKES 6 SERVINGS

1 teaspoon coconut oil or unsalted butter, melted

16 ounces full-fat cream cheese, at room temperature

2 teaspoons vanilla extract

1 tablespoon grated lemon zest (regular or Meyer lemons), plus more for garnish

1 tablespoon fresh lemon juice (regular or Meyer lemon)

10 to 20 drops of liquid stevia (or keto-friendly sweetener of choice), to taste

2 large eggs, at room temperature

2 cups water

3 tablespoons Lemon Curd (page 168)

MACRONUTRIENTS PER SERVING

CALORIES: 314

FAT: 30 G/267 CALORIES

CARBOHYDRATE: 8 G/30 CALORIES

PROTEIN: 7 G/28 CALORIES

1. Trace the bottom of an insert pan on parchment paper and cut out 2 rounds to fit the pans. Cut 4 more strips of parchment paper that are 1½ inches wide x 12 inches long.

2. Use the coconut oil to grease the insides (bottom and sides) of both pans. Place the parchment rounds in the bottom of the pans and line the inside walls with the strips.

3. In a bowl, with an electric mixer, beat together the cream cheese, vanilla, lemon zest, lemon juice, and 10 drops of stevia. Taste the cheese mixture and add more stevia if desired. It is meant to be a little tart. Add the eggs and beat for 20 to 30 seconds, until totally combined. Do not overmix.

4. Divide the cream cheese mixture evenly between the two pans and tap them gently on the counter. Stack them and secure the lid with the handle. Lower the pans into the Instant Pot.

5. Pour the water into the Instant Pot. Secure the lid and set the steam release valve to Sealing. Press the Pressure Cook or Manual button and set the cook time to 25 minutes.

6. When the Instant Pot beeps, allow the pressure to release naturally for 10 minutes, then carefully switch the steam release valve to Venting. When fully released, open the lid and carefully remove the cheesecakes (they will be hot). Place them on a cooling rack and let rest for 30 minutes.

7. Open the lids and check to see if any water has collected on the surface. If it has, blot it with a clean towel. Re-cover the cheesecakes and refrigerate them until well chilled, at least 4 hours.

8. To serve, carefully invert one of the cheesecakes onto a serving plate. Gently spread the lemon curd over the top. Carefully invert the second cheesecake on top. Garnish with additional lemon zest and serve chilled.

EQUIPMENT

2 (7½-inch-diameter) stackable stainless steel insert pans

FATS & FERMENTATIONS

177

178

182

Oven-roasted garlic can take up to an hour, but this recipe is done in half the time. Use roasted garlic to make Roasted Garlic Compound Butter (opposite) or put it atop any roasted vegetables, blend it into mashed cauliflower, or scramble it in eggs. There is no limit to the ways you will use it!

ROASTED GARLIC

1 head garlic

1 cup water

2 teaspoons extra-virgin olive oil

MACRONUTRIENTS PER 2 CLOVES

CALORIES: 22

FAT: 2 G/14 CALORIES

CARBOHYDRATE: 2 G/8 CALORIES

PROTEIN: <1 G/2 CALORIES

1. Slice off the top ¼ inch of the garlic head to expose the cloves and place inside a small ramekin. Pour the water into the Instant Pot. Place the metal steam rack/trivet inside. Set the ramekin on the rack. Secure the lid and set the steam release valve to Sealing. Press the Pressure Cook or Manual button and set the cook time to 25 minutes.

2. When the Instant Pot beeps, carefully switch the steam release valve to Venting to quick-release the pressure. When fully released, open the lid. Use tongs to carefully lift out the ramekin (it will be hot).

3. Position an oven rack to a middle position, about 10 inches below the heating element, and set the oven broiler to low. If the ramekin is not broilerproof, transfer the garlic to a broilerproof pan. Drizzle the garlic with the olive oil and broil, keeping an eye on it, until browned and fragrant, about 3 minutes.

This garlic butter can dress up practically anything. A slice of garlic butter and some Gorgonzola crumbles can take a plain steak from good to phenomenal. Make big batches and freeze individual portions so you always have some on hand.

ROASTED GARLIC COMPOUND BUTTER

MAKES A GENEROUS ½ CUP

1   head Roasted Garlic (opposite)

8   tablespoons (4 ounces) unsalted butter, at room temperature

½   teaspoon sea salt

MACRONUTRIENTS PER 1 GENEROUS TABLESPOON (⅛ OF RECIPE)

CALORIES: 118

FAT: 13 G/114 CALORIES

CARBOHYDRATE: 2 G/6 CALORIES

PROTEIN: <1 G/2 CALORIES

1. Separate the cloves of roasted garlic and squeeze the contents out into a bowl. Add the softened butter and salt. Using a hand mixer, beat until the garlic is smooth and the butter is whipped, 2 to 3 minutes.

2. Transfer the butter to a piece of wax paper and shape into a small loaf. Roll tightly, then place in the freezer for 45 minutes to 1 hour to firm up. Cut into slices and store in an airtight container in the refrigerator or freezer.

Ghee is a fantastic source of healthy fat that is common in Indian and other regional cuisines. Ghee is simply butter that has been clarified, meaning the milk proteins, and hence most of the lactose present in butter, are removed. This is great news for individuals who do not tolerate dairy. Many lactose-intolerant folks can consume ghee with no ill effects. If you are dairy-free and missing butter, try ghee! Also try my turmeric-infused variation (opposite), which makes use of two health-promoting and delicious super-stars, turmeric and cardamom.

GHEE

MAKES ABOUT 1½ CUPS

1   pound unsalted butter, preferably grass-fed

MACRONUTRIENTS PER 1 TABLESPOON

CALORIES: 112

FAT: 13 G/112 CALORIES

CARBOHYDRATE: 0 G/0 CALORIES

PROTEIN: 0 G/0 CALORIES

1. Set the Instant Pot to Sauté. Add the butter and cook, stirring occasionally, for 7 to 9 minutes. When the ghee first begins to cook, it will splatter and pop as the water cooks off. If you have a splatter screen, you can lay it across the top of your pot to protect your counters. Next, the butter will separate into three layers with milk solids on the bottom, clarified butter (ghee) in the center, and foam on the top. Once the ghee separates, allow it to cook for 1 to 2 minutes longer or until the milk solids have just begin to caramelize. For nuttier-tasting ghee, cook 30 seconds to 1 minute longer.

2. Press Cancel. Carefully remove the pot insert to stop the cooking process. Skim the foam from the top and discard it.

3. Allow the ghee to cool in the pot until safe to handle, about 5 minutes.

4. When the ghee has cooled, line a fine-mesh sieve with two layers of cheesecloth and carefully strain the ghee into airtight storage containers, leaving the milk solids in the pot. Ghee can be stored at room temperature for up to 1 month or in the refrigerator for 6 months.

TURMERIC-INFUSED GHEE

Make the ghee as directed through step 1. After you skim the foam in step 2, add 1 teaspoon ground turmeric and 2 to 3 whole cardamom pods to the pot. Return the insert to the Instant Pot and press the Slow Cook button. Adjust the temperature to Normal and allow the spices to infuse for 20 minutes. Press Cancel. Continue with the ghee steps 3 and 4.

YOGURT

Making homemade yogurt allows you to enjoy yogurt with full control over the ingredients. You can avoid the thickeners, sweeteners, and artificial ingredients included in many commercial yogurts. Additionally, it gives you the ability to be particular about the quality of the milk used.

Yogurt is a fermented food—excellent for gut health! Beneficial bacteria are an important part of the preparation. There are two main options for inoculating your yogurt with bacteria: The first is to simply use off-the-shelf probiotic supplement capsules or powder. The second is to use a yogurt starter culture, which can be readily purchased online or in most health food stores and co-ops (check the refrigerated cases). The latter option will allow for the greatest control over taste and consistency, as different bacterial strains have different characteristics. Yogurt starter cultures also allow you to experiment with "heirloom" varieties of yogurt such as Bulgarian or Greek. If you are using a yogurt starter culture, be sure to select a culture listed as being "thermophilic" (meaning heat-loving), as you will be incubating your yogurt at around 110°F. Mesophilic (meant for countertop incubation) cultures may not survive a heated incubation process.

HOMEMADE DAIRY YOGURT

MAKES ABOUT 4 CUPS

1 cup water

1 quart whole milk (see Note, page 185)

1 packet yogurt starter culture (recommended) or 1 teaspoon powdered probiotics

1. Sanitize all equipment that will come in contact with your yogurt, such as jars, lids, mixing utensils, and thermometer.

2. Pour the water into the Instant Pot. Place the metal steam rack/trivet inside. Evenly divide the milk between several mason jars or heatproof glass containers, leaving about ½ inch of headspace at the top: two pint jars or four half-pint jars work well for this. To prevent condensation from dripping into the milk, set the lids atop the jars without sealing or cover with foil.

3. Secure the lid of the Instant Pot and set the steam release valve to Sealing. Select Steam and set the cook time for 2 minutes. When the Instant Pot beeps, allow the pressure to release naturally for 10 minutes, then carefully switch the steam release valve to Venting to quick-release the pressure. When fully released, open the lid. Using tongs or oven mitts, very carefully lift the lids off the jars and check that the temperature of the milk has reached 180°F. If the temperature is too low, you can continue to Steam in 2-minute increments until 180°F is reached.

4. When the milk has reached 180°F, use canning tongs or oven mitts to very carefully lift the jars out of the Instant Pot (they will be hot) and place them on a rack to cool undisturbed until the milk temperature falls to 110° to 100°F (use a digital thermometer to monitor it). If you wish to shorten the cooling time, once the jars have cooled on the rack for about 5 minutes, you may set the containers inside a bowl of cold water. Add a cupful of ice cubes to the water and stir the milk gently until the proper temperature is reached. Do not allow water to get in the milk.

5. When the milk has reached the correct temperature range, remove any skin that has formed on top of the milk and discard. Evenly distribute the starter culture granules among the jars and stir well. Return the jars to the Instant Pot and once again place the lids on the jars without sealing.

6. Secure the lid of the Instant Pot. Press the Yogurt button and set the fermentation time to 8 hours (see Note). The LCD screen will read "Yogt" when complete. Carefully remove the jars and let cool, then secure the lids and transfer to the refrigerator.

7. If you wish to make Greek-style yogurt, pour the finished yogurt into a nut milk bag or a cheesecloth-lined sieve set over a bowl. Allow the whey to drain out for 10 hours or longer until the desired consistency is reached.

MACRONUTRIENTS PER ¼ CUP

CALORIES: 37	STRAINED GREEK-STYLE
FAT: 2 G/18 CALORIES	CALORIES: 71
CARBOHYDRATE: 3 G/10 CALORIES	FAT: 6 G/53 CALORIES
PROTEIN: 2 G/9 CALORIES	CARBOHYDRATE: 3 G/10 CALORIES
	PROTEIN: 2 G/9 CALORIES

NOTE: An 8-hour incubation time is provided as a starting point. If you prefer tangier, thicker yogurt, you can experiment with longer incubation times. If you are using an heirloom variety starter culture, refer to the incubation instructions provided by the culture's manufacturer.

Coconut yogurt is made essentially the same way as dairy yogurt, with a few small changes. Because coconut yogurt does not thicken on its own, gelatin is added at the end.

HOMEMADE COCONUT YOGURT

MAKES ABOUT 4 CUPS

3   (13.5-ounce) cans full-fat coconut milk

1   cup water

1   packet nondairy yogurt starter culture (recommended), 1 teaspoon powdered probiotics, or 2 tablespoons coconut yogurt

½   tablespoon unflavored gelatin

MACRONUTRIENTS PER ¼ CUP

CALORIES: 125

FAT: 12 G/108 CALORIES

CARBOHYDRATE: 4 G/16 CALORIES

PROTEIN: 1 G/4 CALORIES

NOTE: If you prefer tangier, thicker yogurt, you can experiment with longer incubation times.

1. Sanitize all the equipment that will come in contact with your yogurt, such as jars, lids, mixing utensils, and thermometer.

2. Refrigerate the cans of coconut milk *upside-down* for 1 hour. Take care not to shake the cans or turn them over and carefully open them. Pour off the liquid (save it to use in soups or smoothies), leaving the coconut cream behind.

3. Pour the water into the Instant Pot. Place the metal steam rack/trivet inside. Evenly divide the coconut cream among several mason jars or heatproof glass containers, leaving about ½ inch headspace at the top: two pint jars or four half-pint jars work well for this. To prevent condensation from dripping into the cream, set the lids atop the jars without sealing or cover with foil.

4. Secure the lid of the Instant Pot and set the steam release valve to Sealing. Press the Steam button and set the cook time for 2 minutes.

5. When the Instant Pot beeps, allow the pressure to release naturally for 10 minutes, then carefully switch the steam release valve to Venting to quick-release the pressure. When fully released, open the lid. Using canning tongs or oven mitts, very carefully lift the lids off the jars and check that the temperature of the coconut cream has reached 180°F. If the temperature is too low, you can continue to Steam in 2-minute increments until 180°F is reached.

6. When the coconut cream has reached 180°F, use canning tongs or oven mitts to very carefully lift the jars out of the

Instant Pot (they will be hot). Slowly sprinkle in the gelatin and stir well until fully dissolved. Allow the jars to cool on a rack undisturbed until the coconut cream temperature falls to 110° to 100°F (use a digital thermometer to monitor it). If you wish to shorten the cooling time, once the jars have cooled on the rack for 5 minutes, you may set the containers inside a bowl of cold water. Add a cupful of ice cubes to the water and stir the yogurt gently until the proper temperature is reached. Do not allow water to get in the coconut cream.

7. When the coconut cream has reached the correct temperature range, evenly distribute the starter culture granules among the jars and stir well. Return the jars to the Instant Pot and once again place the lids on the jars without sealing. Secure the lid of the Instant Pot.

8. Press the Yogurt button and set the fermentation time to 8 hours (see Note). The LCD screen will read "Yogt" when complete. Carefully remove the jars and let cool, then secure the lids and place the jars in the refrigerator. The yogurt will thicken as it chills.

This is a delicious and easy way to get more fermented food into your diet. You will need a starter culture to introduce the beneficial bacteria into your cream. I recommend purchasing direct-set crème fraîche starter culture online; it is readily available and will yield the truest flavor. For best results, a digital thermometer is also highly recommended to monitor the temperature of the cream. Use cultured cream in place of kefir or sour cream when making soups, dips, smoothies, and more. Instructions for turning freshly cultured cream into probiotic-rich cultured butter follow!

CULTURED CREAM

MAKES ABOUT 2 CUPS

1 cup water

2 cups heavy whipping cream (see Note)

½ packet direct-set crème fraîche starter culture; or 2 tablespoons yogurt, buttermilk, or prepared crème fraîche

MACRONUTRIENTS PER 1 TABLESPOON

CALORIES: 24

FAT: 2 G/18 CALORIES

CARBOHYDRATE: 1 G/4 CALORIES

PROTEIN: 0 G/0 CALORIES

1. Sanitize all the equipment that will come in contact with your preparation, such as jars, lids, mixing utensils, and thermometer.

2. Pour the water into the Instant Pot. Place the metal steam rack/trivet inside. Pour the cream into a heatproof container. A mason jar works well, but leave at least 1 inch of headspace at the top. To prevent condensation from dripping into the cream, set the lid atop the jar without sealing or cover with foil.

3. Secure the lid of the Instant Pot and set the steam release valve to Sealing. Press the Steam button and set the time to 2 minutes. When the Instant Pot beeps, allow the pressure to release naturally for 10 minutes, then carefully switch the steam release valve to Venting to quick-release the pressure. When fully released, open the lid. Using canning tongs or oven mitts, very carefully lift the lid off the jar and check that the temperature of the cream has reached 180°F. If the temperature is too low, you can continue to Steam in 2-minute increments until 180°F is reached.

4. When the cream has reached 180°F, use canning tongs or oven mitts to very carefully lift the jar out of the Instant Pot (it will be hot). Allow it to cool on a rack for about 5 minutes, then partially submerge it in a dish of ice water. Do not allow the water to enter the jar. Place a digital thermometer inside the jar and gently stir until the temperature falls to 115° to 110°F.

5. When the cream has cooled, add the starter culture and stir well. Return the jar to the Instant Pot and loosely cover again with the lid or foil. Secure the lid of the Instant Pot.

6. Press the Yogurt button and set the fermentation time to 10 hours. The LCD screen will read "Yogt" when complete. (If you are making the cultured butter on page 186, continue on to step 1 of the recipe at this point.) Taste the cultured cream. If you prefer a tangier cream, incubate for an additional 2 hours. Otherwise, store in the refrigerator to use as desired. The cream will thicken as it sits under refrigeration.

NOTE: Avoid ultra-pasteurized (UP) or ultra-high temperature pasteurized (UHT) dairy products as they produce inconsistent results and may not set properly.

CULTURED BUTTER

MAKES ABOUT 1 CUP

Cultured Cream
(page 184)

MACRONUTRIENTS PER 1 TABLESPOON

CALORIES: 100

FAT: 11 G/99 CALORIES

CARBOHYDRATE: 0 G/0 CALORIES

PROTEIN: 0 G/0 CALORIES

1. Make the cultured cream through the beginning of step 6. Transfer to the refrigerator to chill, about 1 hour.

2. Transfer the cream to a bowl. Using a hand mixer, blender, or food processor, mix the cream until it begins to separate into solid butter and liquid buttermilk, 3 to 5 minutes. When this occurs, stop mixing and allow the cream to rest for a minute or two.

3. Set a fine-mesh sieve over a bowl and pour the blended cream through the sieve to separate the buttermilk from the butter. Transfer the butter to a large bowl. Reserve the buttermilk for another use (see Note).

4. To prevent spoilage, any remaining buttermilk should be kneaded out of the butter. To do this, pour fresh water over the butter and knead the butter in the bowl with a spatula or clean hands. The water will become cloudy. Pour off the water and add fresh water, kneading again and pouring off the cloudy water. Continue this process several times until the water remains clear.

5. Stir in any herbs and spices you want. Transfer the butter to an airtight container, or wrap it tightly in wax paper. It will stay good in the refrigerator for several weeks at least.

NOTE: You can use the buttermilk to start another fermentation process such as a new batch of cultured cream, or drink it or add it to smoothies for a dose of beneficial probiotics.

It can be difficult to find store-bought ricotta that doesn't also include a long list of stabilizers in the ingredients. This simple, three-step recipe allows you to make rich, fresh ricotta at home.

HOMEMADE RICOTTA

MAKES ABOUT 2 CUPS

8 cups whole milk (see Note)

1 cup heavy whipping cream

½ teaspoon sea salt

2 tablespoons fresh lemon juice, plus more if necessary

MACRONUTRIENTS PER ¼ CUP

CALORIES: 107

FAT: 8 G/72 CALORIES

CARBOHYDRATE: 2 G/8 CALORIES

PROTEIN: 7 G/28 CALORIES

1. Pour the milk, cream, and salt into the Instant Pot. Secure the lid and select the Yogurt setting and adjust until "Boil" is displayed. This will scald the milk, which is what you want. When the program completes, carefully remove the hot insert from the Instant Pot.

2. Add the lemon juice to the scalded milk and stir the milk once or twice *slowly* and with care. The acid from the lemon juice will cause the milk to curdle. If this does not occur after a few minutes, add more lemon juice, 2 tablespoons at a time, and stir again, slowly. Let the mixture rest for 5 minutes.

3. Set a fine-mesh sieve over a large bowl and line it with several layers of cheesecloth. Slowly pour the milk through the sieve to drain for 30 minutes or longer, until the desired consistency is reached. (Reserve the whey that collects in the bowl for another use if desired.)

4. Scoop the ricotta out of the strainer and transfer to an airtight container. Store in the refrigerator for up to 2 weeks.

NOTE: Avoid UHT or ultra-pasteurized milk, and seek out more minimally pasteurized or raw milk instead. Although UHT milk will still set and the taste will be unaffected, the texture may suffer. UHT milk tends to produce smaller curds and yield less ricotta.

INDEX

Note: Page references in *italics* indicate photographs.

T

Tomato(es)
  Chicken Tinga, 150
  Red Sauce, 93
  Sausage and Peppers, *154, 155*
Turmeric
  Golden Cauliflower Rice, 37
  -Infused Ghee, 179, *179*

V

Vegetables. *See specific vegetables*

W

Walnut(s)
  Lemon Garlic Tomato Chicken, 126–27, *127*
  Savory Beet and Basil Parfait, 94–95
Whipped Cream, Basic, 163

Y

Yogurt, 180
  Homemade Coconut, 182–83, *183*
  Homemade Dairy, 180–81

Sauce, Herby, 156
Savory Beet and Basil Parfait, 94–95

Z

Zucchini
  Beef Pho (Pho Bo), 76–77, *78–79*
  Creamy Shrimp Primavera, 151
  Moroccan-Spiced, 104

About the Authors

MARK SISSON is the author of the *New York Times* bestseller *The Keto Reset Diet* and numerous other bestselling books about the primal and keto lifestyle. His blog, MarksDailyApple.com, is one of the most-visited health information websites on the Internet, lauded for challenging and reshaping flawed conventional wisdom about diet, exercise, and lifestyle. Mark's Primal Blueprint enterprise encompasses print and online educational materials, a health coach certification program, and a line of healthy kitchen products and nutritional supplements. Mark, sixty-four, has a BA in biology from Williams College and is a former world-class endurance athlete, with a 2:18 marathon and a fourth-place finish in the Hawaii Ironman World Triathlon Championships to his credit. He lives in Miami, Florida, and holds his own every weekend in high-stakes Ultimate Frisbee matches with hotshots half his age.

LINDSAY TAYLOR, Ph.D., is the Senior Writer and Researcher at Primal Blueprint Publishing. An ultrarunner and Ironman triathlon finisher, Lindsay is an expert in preparing low-carb, nutrient-dense food to fuel her on and off the racecourse. She has been the lead consultant, editor, and recipe tester for several of Mark Sisson's bestselling books. A social/personality psychologist by training, she brings her expertise to bear on topics related to mind-set, goal setting, and lifestyle change as a contributor to the *Primal Blueprint* and *Primal Endurance* podcasts and as the founder and lead moderator of the thriving Keto Reset and Primal Endurance communities on Facebook. She lives in Northern California with her husband and two boys, where she attempts to model a healthy, balanced approach to endurance training, work, and family. Find her healthy, colorful meal creations on her Instagram @theusefuldish.

LAYLA McGOWAN began cooking at an early age as her mother introduced her to the Korean recipes that had been passed down orally through her family for generations. In her mother's kitchen she grew to appreciate that food can simultaneously provide bodily healing, give daily nourishment, and be an expression of true joy. From those roots, Layla has evolved a lifestyle of diverse culinary, health, and fitness practices, motivating and inspiring others in and out of the kitchen. She is an avid weightlifter and is known to her neighbors as the strange woman who practices yoga on the lawn. Layla lives in Alabama with her husband, Ryan. Get inspired by her fitness goals and kitchen creations on Instagram @strong.and.wellfed.